CHAMPIONS OF FREEDOM
Volume 44

Money:
History and Controversies

Gary Wolfram, Editor

Hillsdale College Press
Hillsdale, Michigan 49242

Hillsdale College Press

CHAMPIONS OF FREEDOM
The Ludwig von Mises Lecture Series—Volume 44
Money: History and Controversies

© 2016 Hillsdale College Press, Hillsdale, Michigan 49242

First printing 2016

The views expressed in this volume are not necessarily the views of Hillsdale College.

Printed in the United States of America

Front cover: © design by A. Donley

Library of Congress Control Number: 2016953499

ISBN: 978-1-941946-24-4

Contents

Recommended Readings

Acknowledgment

The publication of this volume was made possible by a generous gift from the Alwin C. Carus Coin Collection Endowment.

Contributors

Kenneth Calvert is associate professor of history at Hillsdale College and headmaster at Hillsdale Academy. He holds degrees from Wheaton College, Gordon-Conwell Theological Seminary, Harvard University, and Miami University of Ohio. He teaches courses on ancient Roman, Greek, Mesopotamian, and Christian history, and, since 2006, he has served on the Alwin Carus Coin Collection Committee. He is a recipient of the Emily Daughtrey Award for Teaching Excellence, and he has been voted Professor of the Year. He has written on various topics touching on ancient history and classical education.

Robert Barro is Paul M. Warburg Professor of Economics at Harvard University, a senior fellow of the Hoover Institution of Stanford University, and a research associate of the National Bureau of Economic Research. He earned his Ph.D. in economics from Harvard University. He is co-editor of Harvard's *Quarterly Journal of Economics.* He has served as president of the Western Economic Association and vice president of the American Economic Association. He is the author or co-author of a number of books, including, *Macroeconomics: A Modern Approach, Economic Growth, Nothing Is Sacred: Economic Ideas for the New Millennium,* and *Getting It Right: Markets and Choices in a Free Society.*

John Steele Gordon, who was educated at Vanderbilt University, is a historian and journalist. His articles have appeared in numerous publications, including *Forbes*, *Commentary*, the *New York Times*, and *The Wall Street Journal*. He is a contributing editor at *American Heritage*, where he wrote the "Business of America" column for many years. He currently writes "The Long View" column for *Barron's*. He is the author of several books, including *Hamilton's Blessing: The Extraordinary Life and Times of Our National Debt*, *The Great Game: The Emergence of Wall Street as a World Power*, and *An Empire of Wealth: The Epic History of American Economic Power*.

Peter Schiff is the CEO and Chief Global Strategist of Euro Pacific Capital. He earned a degree in finance and accounting from U.C. Berkeley. He served as an economic advisor to Ron Paul in the 2008 presidential campaign. Widely quoted in such publications as *The Wall Street Journal*, *Barron's*, *Investor's Business Daily*, the *Financial Times*, and the *New York Times*, he is a frequent guest on CNBC, CNN, Fox News, and the Fox Business Network. He is the author of numerous books, including *How an Economy Grows and Why it Crashes* and *The Real Crash: America's Coming Bankruptcy—How to Save Yourself and Your Country*.

William Walton is the managing partner of Rappahannock Ventures, Rush River Entertainment, and The Forge Studios. He is also vice president of the Council for National Policy and a senior fellow at the Discovery Institute's Center on Wealth, Poverty & Morality. A former director of the U.S. Chamber of Commerce, he earned his B.S. and M.B.A at Indiana University. He has served as chairman of the board and CEO of Allied Capital Corporation and also as managing director of Butler Capital Corporation. He serves on several boards of directors, including the Heritage Foundation, the Media Research Center, and For America.

Introduction

It is too bad that Ludwig von Mises was not alive to take part in the November 2015 Center for Constructive Alternatives conference, "Money: History and Controversies." Beginning with his 1912 book, *The Theory of Money and Credit*, Mises examined how money came into existence and developed the Austrian Business Cycle Theory to explain how the artificial expansion of credit, often undertaken today as a matter of policy by central banks, can lead to booms that are followed by the resulting but necessary busts.

In *Human Action*, Mises discussed how entrepreneurs make decisions about whether to produce consumer goods today or to use the resources to produce capital goods that will produce consumer goods in the future. The signal to the entrepreneur to invest in capital goods rather than to produce consumer goods is the interest rate. A low interest rate implies consumers are saving and investment should take place, since the resources are available to produce the capital goods today, and consumers will be able to purchase the consumer goods in the future. When the central bank keeps interest rates below their natural rate, it leads to mal-investment—the production of capital goods that will not be used efficiently—because the demand for the consumer products will not be there in the future.

The result is an artificial boom, misallocated capital, and an eventual bust as resources must move to those sectors where there is in fact demand. The recent Great Recession certainly fits this description with housing serving as the malinvestment. Mises argued that the longer a central bank attempts to keep a downturn from happening, the greater the recession will be. His primary point is that the problem of business cycles is not due to the fact that capitalism is unstable but rather to government intervention in money and credit.

The authors of this volume cover a range of Mises's interests. Ken Calvert and John Steele Gordon give us a history of money and banking, while Robert Barro, William Walton, and Peter Schiff discuss the economic and political effects of government debt and monetary policy.

In his essay, "The History of Money," Ken Calvert provides not only a walk-through of the history of money, but discusses the role money has played in the development of civilization. Calvert points out, in concert with Mises, that money is not restricted to particular pieces of paper certified by government, but rather can be anything that serves as a medium of exchange. Metal coins became a dominant form of money because they have characteristics that make them a natural medium of exchange. Included among these features is that they are scarce, valuable, durable, and can be formed and shaped. He discusses how the development of money and its ability to reduce the cost of exchange contributed to the advancement of civilization.

Calvert then examines a number of coins, pointing out the particulars of each coin and how these reflect the governments that issued them and the societies that used them. His discussion inspires the reader to read more ancient history to appreciate the details of how and why these coins came into being. In one example, Calvert notes that Alexander the Great put his own picture on coins to signify his status as a god-man to be revered by anyone using the coin. Calvert closes by showing that the history of money is a mechanism for studying how art, science, and philosophy were able to advance and that money does not by itself lead to evil, but rather to a social order in which charity is made possible.

John Steele Gordon in his essay, "Money in American History," provides a thorough and interesting history of money and the banking system in the United States. He begins with some fascinating observations: How the expression "pieces of eight" came about, why a quarter is also known as two bits, why the American colonies had a variety of different currencies in circulation such as Spanish, French, and Portuguese money, as well as wampum; how a financial crisis helped lead to the Constitutional Convention; why wildcat banks were called wildcat banks; and even how the words Hillsdale and dollar are etymologically linked. He then develops a coherent analysis of the U.S. banking and monetary system and what circumstances led to each stage of its development.

Gordon explains the differences between the philosophies of Thomas Jefferson and Alexander Hamilton with regard to the banking system, and how the colonies were able to develop a currency and fund the War of Independence. He discusses the era from the war with Britain through the veto of the charter for the Second Bank of the Unites States, the era of free banking, the difficulties of funding the Civil War, and the panics of 1893 and 1907. Gordon also considers the Great Depression and the dropping of the gold standard, and culminates with some observations about how credit cards will eventually affect the U.S. monetary system.

Robert Barro's essay, "Milton Friedman and Monetarism," offers a clear analysis of the development of the theory of monetarism from Friedman's early work through the Great Recession, by an author who is ranked among the top macroeconomists in the world.

Barro leads the reader through Friedman's early works, such as *Capitalism and Freedom*, and explains the differences and similarities between monetarist and Keynesian prescriptions for monetary policy. He explains how Friedman arrived at his famous rule that the Federal Reserve should not use discretionary policy but rather should expand the money supply at a constant rate of two to three percent. He notes that if the demand for money is not stable, then this rule won't necessarily provide the price stability that Friedman envisioned.

William Walton's paper, "The Problem of Crony Capitalism Today," discusses how big government serves as a means for big business to restrict competition and procure unjust advantages. This is a problem that is "massive and growing." He argues this is primarily the result of the astounding growth in the federal government, both on the regulatory and tax sides of the economic system. He discusses how this growth of government has undermined the economic and political systems of the country and threatens the "foundations of our culture."

His argument reminds one of Frederic Bastiat's observation in his 1850 book *The Law*—that once the government engages in legalized plunder, the plundered classes will attempt to engage in the making of the law. Walton shows that this was a bipartisan development: following on the heels of the Great Society, the Nixon administration promulgated numerous regulations. Walton discusses the banking and financial regulation sparked by the Great Recession and offers some ways to restore the market system.

Peter Schiff sets out a dismal view of the results of Federal Reserve policy and the consequences of the federal debt burden in his paper, "How to Think About the Federal Reserve." He argues that the Federal Reserve's actions not only were a primary cause of the recent fiscal crisis, but they have generally hampered economic growth. He points out that when the Federal Reserve was created it was not able to purchase federal government debt, since that could enable the federal government to spend well beyond its means. With the fiscal burden of World War I, this restriction was lifted. As a result, the Federal Reserve has contributed significantly to the problem of massive—and growing—federal debt.

Schiff argues that we are headed for a fiscal crisis larger than that of the Great Recession, because the Federal Reserve misunderstands its effects on the economy and will continue policies that will eventually lead to a collapse in demand for U.S. debt and possible hyperinflation. He believes the solution to this problem is an understanding of the root causes of economic downturns and a reduction of the government burdens on our capitalist system.

This CCA lecture series provided timely discussion of important policy questions regarding the proper role of the Federal Reserve and the problems associated with an expanding federal debt. During the Great Recession, the Federal Reserve undertook massive purchases of both government debt and mortgage-backed securities held by the banking system. Meanwhile, federal government expenditures expanded in the belief that government was the answer to economic downturns rather than the cause of them. The Federal Reserve now holds more than $4 trillion in securities, while federal government debt has reached an unprecedented high relative to the national gross domestic product. It is essential to the maintenance of economic and political freedom to restore the proper relationship between government and the free market.

GARY WOLFRAM
William E. Simon Professor of
Economics and Public Policy
Hillsdale College

KENNETH CALVERT

The Origins of Money

Throughout history human beings have used a variety of goods as money. We tend to think of money as coins or pieces of paper, but anything that human beings put a value on and use as a medium of exchange is money. It can be items as different as a chunk of wood or a gold coin. Over time, certain things emerge as more valuable than others, such as gold, silver, bronze, and precious metals generally. These metals are highly valuable and scarce, they can be formed or shaped, and they are durable. Money had its origin in agriculture. For example, a shekel was a weight of grain in the ancient Near East. A scruple was roughly equivalent to one drachma. A drachma is a handful of obols—drachma literally means a handful—and an obol is an iron stick.

In the ancient Roman world *Aes* was a chunk of bronze used for trade [See Fig. 1]. The word money has its origins in the Roman goddess Juno Moneta. Romans forged their coins in her temple, the original Roman mint.

---

*All coins pictured in this essay can be found in the Alwin C. Carus Coin Collection at Hillsdale College.

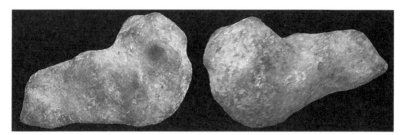

[Fig. 1] Rome, Aes Rude, 3rd Century B.C.

Let's consider some of the things that have been used through-out history as a means of exchange. In ancient China there was Ming Tao, or knife money, that is bronze fashioned in the shape of a knife or sword [See Fig. 2]. In philosophy, Tao means the way, but in its original meaning it referred to a knife or a sword.

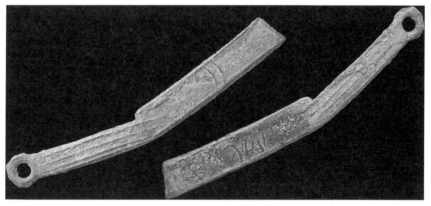

[Fig. 2] China, Ming Tao Knife Money, 400–225 B.C.

Ancient China also had what was known as Pu money [See Fig. 3]. A Pu was a spade, used by farmers. Both of these early coins, the Tao and the Pu were tools and had agricultural roots. Whether we consider China or India or the Mediterranean region, when a people creates a metallic form of money, quite often their currency takes on the form of things that they're already using as trading items. It took hundreds of years for human beings to move from agricultural exchange—from the exchange of grain, or cattle, for example—to the exchange of metallic money. In many ancient cultures, commerce was viewed as an inferior pursuit compared to agriculture.

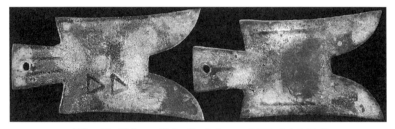

[Fig. 3] China, Chin Pu Money, 255–206 B.C.

Reading the ancient Greeks—such as the historian Hesiod—the early Romans, or the Hebrews of the Old Testament, one finds a suspicion of trade. It took a while for human beings to gain confidence in chunks of metal.

One of the earliest coins is an electrum stator, a coin from the 7th century B.C. in Lydia [See Fig. 4]. The obverse side, or the head of the coin, features the symbol of the royal house of Lydia. Electrum is a naturally occurring alloy of silver and gold, which the royal household of Lydia used to produce some of our earliest known coins. Coinage began in part as a means for governments to pay their debts, but by the 7th century in the Greek world coins began to take on a commercial role. Once coins began to be used in this way, they transformed civilization. Coins make possible many of the great advancements of Western Civilization.

[Fig. 4] Greece, Lydia, Electrum 1/3 Stater, 650–561 B.C.

The city of Aegina, located on the island of Aegina, south of Athens, produced a silver drachma that features an image of a sea turtle on the obverse side [See Fig. 5]. Why a turtle? Aegina was an important sea power, involved in trade and naval activities in the Aegean Sea, and saw itself as a shelled beast in the sea and able to defend itself. Athens later conquered Aegina and forced it to change the sea turtle to a land turtle. The message from Athens was that Aegina belonged to it.

Aegina played a prominent role in the Archaic Age (800–500 B.C.), a period when free trade transformed the world. The various Greek city-states were competing with one another militarily and economically, and creating massive amounts of wealth. This prepared the ground for the invention of Greek philosophy, science, and literature. The idea arose that citizens don't necessarily have to live under a monarch; they could instead be free and self-governing. How were the ancient Greeks able to have the leisure to pursue all of these activities? One important reason is the massive amounts of wealth that were beginning to develop, combined with the fact that the average person could put wealth in his pocket. An average Athenian or Aeginian could carry more wealth in a bag than an aristocrat who owned thousands of acres of land. This transformation in the understanding of wealth had a fundamental impact on the development of Western Civilization.

[Fig. 5] Greece, Aegina, AR Drachm, 510–490 B.C.

One coin from ancient Athens features the head of Athena, the city's goddess, on the obverse side. The reverse side–or what we would call the tail side–has an owl and the word Athens [See Fig. 6]. What is Athens saying about itself? The city is under the authority of its goddess Athena, and the owl is her symbol. Athena is the goddess of wisdom and of war. These particular coins were called owls and were struck in the 5th century—from 499 to 417. Because they were very pure coins with little base alloy added, they were popular throughout the Mediterranean world. One reason why Athens rose to power in the 5th century was because its coinage was trusted. In terms of the history of coinage, the Athenian coin represents purity, a sense of responsibility, and good market value. The Athenians intentionally produced a silver coin of such a quality that it would be used throughout the Mediterranean.

[Fig. 6] Greece, Athens, AR Tetradrachm, 499–417 B.C.

In the ancient world, political communities put their essential convictions on their coins. In a time of widespread illiteracy, citizens at large could know their country's essential principles by looking at their coins. Coins were a very important means of communication.

Alexander the Great minted a coin that features his own visage [See Fig. 7]. What does such a coin say about Alexander the Great's essential convictions? Because his image is on the obverse side, Alexander is saying that he is the most important figure for anyone using his coin. On his head is the skin of the Nemean Lion, which he had killed and which had become his symbol. Alexander equated himself with Hercules, whose first labor was slaying a lion. The coin suggests that Alexander, like Hercules, is a god-man. On the coin's reverse side, Zeus is seated on his throne, and the word Alexander is next to him. As indicated by the coin, Alexander believed that Zeus was his father. Compare Alexander's coin with the Athenian coin, or with the Aeginian. The coins point us to the difference between a free society and a society ruled by a monarch. As coins become a popular medium of exchange, they begin to express the principles at the heart of the society that produces them.

[Fig. 7] Macedonia, Alexander the Great, AR Tetradrachm, 336–323 B.C.

Let's turn to a Roman coin, the Didrachm-Quadrigatus [See Fig. 8]. On the obverse side is Janus, the double-headed god, the god of war, who faces both forward and backward. This coin was minted towards the end of the First Punic War and was also used in the

Second Punic War, both fought against Carthage. The Punic Wars transformed Rome into a powerful force in the central and western Mediterranean. This coin was used to pay for its military activities. On the reverse side of the coin is a *quadriga* or four-horsed chariot of victory and the goddess Roma. The coin suggests that the Romans are dedicated to the victory of Rome in the name of their gods. The coin represents the Senate and people of Rome, that is, the entire republic. There is no human head on it, as we saw with Alexander.

[Fig. 8] Rome, Didrachm-Quadrigatus, 225–212 B.C.

Now consider a coin of the late Roman Republic, known as the coin of Titus Tatius [See Fig. 9]. It was minted on the authority of the Senate.On the obverse side is pictured an old Sabine king, Titus Tatius, who unified with Romulus, the mythical founder of Rome, and in so doing brought their war to an end. They put aside their differences and united against common enemies. Why did the Romans of 66 B.C. mint a coin that emphasized an enemy king, a Sabine, who joined forces with Romulus? In 66 B.C. the Roman Republic was in crisis as Pompey the Great and Crassus fought for political power and control. In an effort to foster unity, the Roman Senate created the Titus Tatius coin as an example of how two mortal enemies could put aside their differences and join together for the good of Rome.

[Fig. 9] Rome, Titus Tatius, Serrate Denarius, 66 B.C.

Julius Caesar produced a coin in 49 B.C., the year he crossed the Rubicon and went to war against Pompey and the Senate [See Fig. 10]. That year marked the beginning of the end of the Roman Republic, which is what this coin represents. This coin does not honor the Roman gods, or the great men of the Roman past. It honors one man: Julius Caesar. There is an elephant on the obverse side, and it is crushing a snake. That is, Ceasar the elephant is crushing his enemy, the Gauls. The reverse side shows the tools of the Pontifex Maximus. In 49 B.C. Caesar held that office and had the tools of religious authority. Not only is Caesar crushing his opponents, he is doing it as a kind of holy war.

[Fig. 10] Roman Republic, Julius Caesar, Denarius, 49–48 B.C.

A coin from the time of the Emperor Claudius—known as a Dupondius—featured the head of Augustus on the obverse side and the divine Augusta, his wife, on the reverse side [See Fig. 11]. By this time Augustus and his wife had been divinized. The gods of Rome had been replaced by human beings who were treated as gods, just as happened in Greece with Alexander the Great.

[Fig. 11] Rome, Augustus, AE Dupondius, 41–42 A.D.

Next Pontius Pilate of Judea minted the "lituus" coin, which reflects a Roman influence [See Fig. 12]. There is no human head on this coin, because that would have been seen as paganism in Judea. The local Jewish population would not have accepted that. Instead, on the obverse side there is a lituus—a stick with a curve at the end that was used by Roman augurs to foretell the future. On the reverse side is a laurel wreath. Pontius Pilate minted these coins so that they could be used throughout the Jewish world. It was no coincidence that the lituus used by pagan augurs could also be interpreted as Moses' staff, and therefore the coin could be seen as a representation of the Jewish exodus from Egypt.

[Fig. 12] Roman Empire, Judea, Pontius Pilate, "Lituus" coin, 31 B.C.

In the sixth century A.D., Justinian I of the Byzantine Empire minted a coin whose obverse side featured the head of Justinian placed over a conquered subject [See Fig. 13]. On the reverse side is an angel holding a sword in his right hand and an orb with a cross in his left, which represents the domination of Christianity over the world. This coin communicates to the Byzantine people that Justinian is the ruler over this world, that he is attempting to reconquer much of the Roman Empire that was lost, and that he is doing it in the name of Christianity.

[Fig. 13] Byzantine Empire, Justinian I, AV Solidus, 527–565 A.D.

Much later, in 1808, the East India Company of Great Britain minted a coin meant to be used in India [See Fig. 14]. It says in Persian on the back that it is produced under the patronage of the King and Parliament of England. Although it is a privately minted coin, it reminds those who use it that they are a part of the British Empire.

[Fig. 14] Great Britain, English East India Company CU 10 Cash, 1808 A.D.

Turning to American coinage, consider the 1874 gold liberty head, a three-cent coin [See Fig. 15]. Today, we think a three-penny coin odd, but at the time these were used to buy the three-cent stamps then in circulation. What does this coin say about America? In the first place, it is made of gold, a precious metal, not a base one. On the obverse side is a Liberty Head, the head of an Indian princess. On the reverse side is a laurel wreath, a wreath of victory. Native Americans have always been portrayed as noble and courageous on American coins, and have served as a representation of liberty.

[Fig. 15] United States Liberty Head, AV Three Dollar Coin, 1874

In conclusion, human beings by nature seek to exchange goods and services with one another. Humans will always seek to better themselves, their families, and their communities, and exchange makes this possible. Exchange is an essential aspect of happy human existence. The more free we are and the greater liberty we have to enter into commerce with one another, the more art, the more science, and the more great ideas will be produced. Does money necessarily lead to great evil? Only if money is your god. In response to that, I often think of something Margaret Thatcher once said: "No one would remember the Good Samaritan if he'd only had good intentions. He had money as well."

ROBERT BARRO

Milton Friedman and Monetarism

Despite his fame in the macroeconomic area—my focus in this essay—Milton Friedman's most important contributions to the policy debate are actually on the microeconomic side. His over-arching theme is the benefits from free markets and private enterprise. The conceptual framework is in the outstanding 1953 book, *Essays in Positive Economics*. Many of the policy proposals were expressed as early as the 1950s and appeared in *Capitalism and Freedom*. This 1962 book—developed from a series of lectures given in 1956— is the classic work on economic ideas for a general audience, and I learn something every time I reread this remarkable work.

Capitalism and Freedom expressed numerous policy ideas once thought to be radical but now viewed as mainstream. The all-volunteer army has worked well in the United States and other countries for many years, privatized social security lives in Chile and elsewhere, the U.S. earned-income tax credit is a form of negative income tax, the flat-rate income tax prevails in Russia and Massachusetts and some other places, school vouchers work in many U.S. localities, and market-oriented welfare reform was enacted by Bill Clinton of all people. In addition, open capital markets are the norm in the developed world, and flexible exchange rates prevail in many countries. Friedman's ideas on the decriminalization of drugs—expressed later on—seem now to be moving toward acceptance. And, finally, there is the strong argument for monetary stability, which has taken hold in its modern form of inflation targeting, though not in his constant-growth-rate-rules for monetary aggregates.

Friedman laid out his academic views on money in "The Quantity of Money—A Restatement" (an essay in the 1956 book, *Studies in the Quantity Theory of Money*) and the epic *A Monetary History of the United States* (written in 1963 with Anna Schwartz). Key features of the quantity theory of money—later referred to as "monetarism"—were, first, that the nominal quantity of money was determined, in many circumstances, independently of the real quantity demanded and, second, that the real demand for money was a stable function of a few key variables, such as real income and the nominal interest rate.

The *Monetary History* explored money-supply determination under different historical regimes, including the gold standard. Friedman and Schwartz argued that much of the observed variation in money supply was independent of shifts in the demand for money. They used this finding to argue that the positive association between nominal money and real economic activity reflected substantial causation from money to the real economy, rather than the reverse.

The odd thing from a current perspective is that Friedman's stress on monetary disturbances was viewed in the 1960s as anti-Keynesian. It is true that Keynes in his *General Theory* deemphasized monetary disturbances as a source of business fluctuations, and he was also skeptical about the role of monetary policy as an anti-recession device. However, particularly since the 1980s, self-styled New Keynesians have embraced activist monetary policy as a centerpiece of counter-cyclical policy. Thus, Friedman's stress on the business-cycle effects of monetary shocks fits comfortably—maybe too comfortably—with Keynesian thinking.

Friedman refined his approach to monetary policy in his 1967 presidential address to the American Economic Association (AEA).

"The Role of Monetary Policy," which appeared in the 1968 *American Economic Review*, is probably the most important contribution ever to come from this format. Usually, presidential addresses and similar speeches cannot be forgotten too soon. A key result—which, along with work by Edmund Phelps, foreshadowed the 1970s Bob Lucas-led revolution on rational expectations macroeconomics—was that only unanticipated movements in money and the price level mattered for real economic activity. However, Milton's monetary framework implied a potentially important role for activist monetary policy in smoothing out the business cycle. Systematic monetary changes had substantial short-term real effects, and wise interventions could improve the functioning of the macro economy. Implicitly, the private market was working badly, beset by sticky prices and wages in the short run, and the monetary authority could help by stimulating the economy in recessions and cooling things down in booms. No wonder that this part of Friedman's monetary ideas would be embraced by Keynesians in the 1980s.

To go from Friedman's monetary framework to an argument for monetary stability, one needs additional features, such as the "long and variable lags" stressed in his *A Program for Monetary Stability*. Even more important is the distinction between rules and authorities emphasized by Henry Simons (and subsequently analyzed in a large literature on rules versus discretion). Models with these features can explain why monetary activism often causes more harm than good, even when (or, rather, especially if) monetary shocks have major real effects. Thus, these extensions can reconcile Friedman's conceptual framework with the constant-growth-rate rules for monetary aggregates that he favored in practical policy advice.

Friedman was very successful with the broad proposition that monetary policy activism tends to be mistaken. However, his well-known, specific proposal—that a monetary aggregate such as M1 or M2 grow at a pre-specified rate such as 2 or 3% per year—has problems. In fact, this area is the only one I know of where he pretty much reversed his previous position. The problem is that the real demand for money is not that stable. This instability was apparent in seasonal fluctuations before the establishment of the Federal Reserve in 1913. However, the instability applies also to seasonally-adjusted data, as became clear recently with the dramatic run-up of U.S. real monetary aggregates, especially those related to the monetary base (currency plus deposits held at the Federal Reserve). Therefore, a constant growth rate for any monetary aggregate does not ensure anything close to inflation stability. One way or another, a monetary policy aimed at inflation stability has to allow the nominal quantity of money to adjust to shifts in the real quantity of money demanded.

Inflation targeting is such a system and has been adopted by many central banks—though this system has been seriously challenged in recent years by the persistence of short-term nominal interest rates close to the lower bound around zero. Under inflation targeting, nominal interest rates react positively to deviations of inflation from target. This system has been pursued in an implicit form by the Federal Reserve since the mid-1980s and in explicit forms by New Zealand and numerous other central banks since 1989. (Aside from the United States, notable holdouts from explicit inflation targeting are the central banks of the European Union and Japan.) As part of the targeting process, nominal money adjusts automatically to shifts in real money demand. (In technical jargon, the nominal quantity of money is endogenous.) However, this mechanism fails when, as at present, the usual inflation-targeting response calls for declines in nominal interest rates below zero.

It's true that the interest-rate reaction functions of many modern central banks, including the Fed, have encompassed responses of interest rates to variables other than inflation. Notably, in the United States, interest rates have tended to rise when the labor market is tight (gauged by high employment growth and a low unemployment rate), and vice versa. I am unsure whether this part of monetary policy has been useful—but it is apparently not so harmful and does not compromise much the objective of achieving low and stable inflation. In any event, although the refinements since the 1980s in monetary policy are important, the general spirit of the approach fits with Friedman's idea that the major mission of central banks is to ensure low and stable inflation.

Inflation targeting in various forms was enormously successful since the late 1980s, resulting in a great reduction in the mean and variability of inflation in advanced countries and parts of the rest of the world. However, with U.S. and other nominal interest rates remaining close to zero for the last few years, it became infeasible to engineer further reductions in rates in order to offset a tendency for deflation. In response, there has been some shift back to regimes focused on monetary aggregates, such as the several rounds of quantitative easing engaged in by the Federal Reserve. Under this system, the Fed expands the monetary base and, in exchange, acquires assets for its balance sheet. Immediately following the financial crisis of 2008–09, the assets were primarily mortgage-backed securities—not the traditional area of involvement for the Fed and surely a bad idea in terms of the government effectively subsidizing chosen private-sector activities. Subsequently, quantitative easing concentrated on the traditional form of U.S. Treasury securities, particularly longer-term bonds. However, any month now, the Fed will actually raise short-term nominal interest rates and, thereby, move finally away from the zero lower bound and back toward more traditional inflation targeting.

Anyone who wants to understand Friedman's policy ideas should start with *Capitalism and Freedom* and then go to *Free to Choose*, the bestselling 1980 book, which accompanied the television show that made him a household name. He notes in his autobiography—*Two Lucky People: Memoirs*, written in 1998 with his wife, Rose—that France was the only European country never to air the television program. It seems that some things never change.

One thing I learned from the *Memoirs* is that Friedman's policy influence was achieved mainly through the force of ideas, not by direct involvement in government. Except for work in 1935–37 in New Deal Washington (when Milton had no academic job opportunities) and during World War II, he avoided public service. His key advice to academic economists: "…by all means spend a few years in Washington—but only a few. If you stay more than two or three years you will become addicted and will be unable effectively to return to a scholarly career." My only disagreement is that two or three years in Washington are too many.

In any event, Friedman probably would not have been an outstanding policymaker. His main output in Washington during World War II involved work on the establishment of income-tax withholding. It may be that no other law has done more to enlarge the size of the federal government. Certainly he regretted the existence of income-tax withholding, but he also pointed out (no doubt correctly) that this institution would be present even if he had never set foot in Washington. It would, however, have been exciting to have seen Friedman functioning in government as chair of the Federal Reserve. (Would the minutes of every meeting say that we have decided to expand M2 at an annual rate of 3%, followed by a quick adjournment?)

Also in the *Memoirs* is verification of a well-known story about Friedman's concern as 1967 AEA president about the association's accumulation of a substantial surplus. He worried that the money would be spent on ill-advised projects designed by a social do-gooder. Therefore, he successfully proposed the startup of a new journal (the *Journal of Economic Literature*) without an increase in membership dues. The resulting budget deficit used up the endowment in a reasonably quick and nearly harmless manner.

I remembered this episode when I was AEA vice president in 1998. Again, the association had accumulated a large surplus, and I worried about the potential ill-advised uses. My proposal at the time (when the AEA already had three journals) was to cut the membership dues until the endowment declined to a reasonable level. Unfortunately, lacking Friedman's talents at persuasion, I failed miserably in this proposal. I should point out, however, that my proposal for a large cut in dues was eventually enacted, though long after I was an officer. Nevertheless, the Association has again accumulated a lot of money—$32 million at the end of 2014, while still running a surplus—so there is an enduring cause for concern.

Friedman is often cited, starting with *Time* magazine in December 1965, for the famous quote: "We are all Keynesians now." However, we learn from the *Memoirs* that the quote was taken out of context to change the meaning. The full statement as reconstructed by Friedman in a letter to *Time* in 1966 is: "In one sense we are all Keynesians now; in another, nobody is any longer a Keynesian." He explained that the first sense refers to the rhetoric and style of macroeconomic analysis—Keynes essentially invented macroeconomics as a distinct field. The second sense applied to substantive implications; specifically, to the idea that (almost) no one now advocates the simplistic policy activism recommended in Keynes's *General Theory*. Although the second observation is more significant, the first one got most of the press.

I remember seeing Milton and Rose in the summer of 2006, when they were walking on the steps by Stanford's Hoover Institution. For some reason, he told me that he was surprised to be still alive and that he had not planned properly for lasting until age 94. Then, later that summer, I saw him for the last time in San Francisco at a party hosted by George Shultz, fellow of the Hoover Institution and former Secretary of State among other things. The party was in honor of Tony Blair, who was probably scouting out future employment opportunities. There were many prominent people present, and I recall asking someone: "Do you know who is the most important person in this room?" To the uncertain response, I gave the clear answer, "Milton Friedman."

JOHN STEELE GORDON

Money in American History

The story of money in America is a long history and a distinctly checkered one. And like all good stories, it has a few heroes, such as Alexander Hamilton and J. P. Morgan, and a few villains, especially Thomas Jefferson, whose malignant hatred for commerce and the marketplace in general and banking in particular, transmitted down through the political generations, has visited disaster after disaster on the American monetary system.

By the time the United States was founded in 1776, coins had been money for almost 2500 years. Negotiable banknotes had been in general use for less than a century. But by the last decades of the 18th century, a modern money supply had to have both. And thus we can't talk about the history of American money without talking about the history of American banking, for banknotes put banks in the money business. Banks store money and they loan it, but, most importantly, they create it. With banknotes they created money by printing it. Today they create money by crediting an account with a given sum or loaning money on a credit card. Every time one charges something on a credit card, he is, via his bank, borrowing and thus creating money.

But because banks are in the money business, that makes banking a very peculiar business indeed. Cash on hand, for instance, is an asset in most enterprises; it is usually a liability to a bank because it is owed to the depositors. Loans, on the other hand, are assets because they are owed to the bank.

Further, if an ordinary business goes broke, it is a financial problem for the owners, the employees, and the creditors. But the corporate assets, such as factories, will move to stronger hands and continue to produce. But because banks create money far in excess of their reserves, when a bank goes broke, it can affect the personal economic well-being of nearly everyone in the community or even, if the bank is large enough, the entire country.

That's why banks need very careful supervision. Banks, after all, are owned and run by human beings and when humans have in their hands the awesome power to create money out of thin air, the temptation to abuse that power and create too much will be given into regularly. Anyone who has maxed out a credit card knows that temptation.

But banks have often not been properly supervised over the last 230 years of American history and, as a result, bank failure has been as American as apple pie, at huge cost to the American economy.

The first American bank failure took place in Rhode Island in 1809, when a fraudulent bank capitalized at forty-five dollars issued eight hundred thousand dollars in banknotes, a sum equal to more than seventeen thousand times the resources behind it. The failure of Lehman Brothers in 2008, marked the beginning of the explosive phase of the so-called Great Recession that lingers on to this day.

When the United States achieved its independence from Great Britain in 1783 it lacked a reliable form of money. Britain had forbidden the export of British coins, so while American colonists usually kept their accounts in pounds, shillings, and pence, what circulated in day-to-day transactions was a hodgepodge of Spanish, French,

Portuguese, and some British coins, as well as warehouse certificates for tobacco and other products.

Since the British had also forbidden the creation of banks, paper money was printed by some colonies until the British government forbade that too. (Benjamin Franklin, while printing money for the province of Pennsylvania, came up with several characteristically clever anti-counterfeiting techniques.)

In New York Province and elsewhere, wampum, the form of money used by the Indians, was used in general commerce as well, at least until the 1760s, when a man in New Jersey invented a wampum counterfeiting machine and destroyed the value of the real stuff.

Lacking a banking system and a regular money supply, the Continental Congress had no choice but to pay for much of the Revolution by issuing fiat money, called continentals. Fiat money is money because the government says it is money. If the marketplace disagrees, and it often has, the fiat money will quickly inflate into worthlessness if issued in large quantities. That is what happened to continentals, and the phrase, "not worth a continental," was in the American lexicon for over a hundred years.

After the Revolution, the need to design and then create a national money system was an urgent task of the new nation. The question of what new unit of account to adopt was a complex one because the inhabitants of the various colonies had used so many different, often incommensurate units.

Robert Morris, whose financial legerdemain had done so much to keep the Revolution financially afloat, tried to bridge the differences by finding the lowest common divisor of the monetary units most often encountered in each state. He calculated this to be 1,440th of a Spanish dollar. He proposed that this unit be multiplied by 1000, which would have made the new American monetary unit equal to 25/36ths of a Spanish dollar. Thomas Jefferson, with one of his two good ideas about money, argued instead for just adopting the dollar as the monetary unit.

The origin of the word *dollar* lies in the German word for valley, *tal.* In the 15th century, major silver deposits were discovered in what is now the Czech Republic. In 1519, the owner of these mines, the Graf zu Passaun und Weisskirchen began minting coins from this silver, coins which weighed a Saxon ounce, which is slightly smaller than our ounce. Honest and pure, these coins, called talers—literally "from the valley"—had great acceptance in the marketplace and were imitated by other German rulers. In English, *taler* soon turned into *dollar* just as *tal* had earlier turned into *dale* and *dell*, which interestingly links the word *Hillsdale* and *dollar* etymologically.

The Holy Roman Emperor, Charles V, whose vast dominions as King of Spain included the new silver mines of Mexico and Peru, began to mint similar coins. Thanks to those silver mines, the Spanish dollar became the dominant international currency of its day.

Once the dollar was chosen as the monetary unit, it would have been natural to adopt the clunky British system of dividing the basic unit into twenty smaller units, called shillings, and those into twelve still smaller units, called pence.

But the Spanish dollars in use in the colonies had often been cut into halves, fourths, and eighths, called bits, to make small change (which is why Spanish dollars were often called "pieces of eight" and a quarter is still sometimes referred to as "two bits.") So an octal system of currency would have been a natural idea as well.

Jefferson, however, then had his second, and last, good idea about money: make smaller units decimal fractions of the dollar rather than eighths.

Jefferson pushed for coinage of a half dollar, a fifth, a tenth (for which he actually coined the word *dime*), a twentieth, and a hundredth of a dollar, which he called a "cent," a word that had already been coined by Robert Morris. Congress, however, while adopting the cent, five-cent, dime, and fifty-cent coins advocated by Jefferson, decided to authorize a quarter-dollar coin rather than a twenty-cent one. The quarter, of course, is with us yet, now the last, distant echo of the old octal monetary system of colonial days, since the New York Stock Exchange stopped trading in eighths of a dollar in 1999.

Thomas Jefferson's bright idea for a decimal coinage began to spread around the world, as bright ideas always do. Today every country on earth has a decimal currency system. Even the British finally adopted one in 1971.

Of course, at the time, the United States had very little precious metals from which to mint coins.

It was a desperate post-revolutionary financial crisis that helped bring about the Constitutional Convention of 1787, and rationalizing the new government's finances was the first order of business when it came into being in 1789. That's why the Department of the Treasury had 40 employees and the Department of State only five. When Robert Morris turned down the post of Secretary of the Treasury in order speculate in land (a bad idea—he ended up in debtors' prison), President Washington offered the post to Alexander Hamilton, then only in his early thirties.

Hamilton faced a formidable task and he accomplished it brilliantly, using a bit of political sausage-making to push his plan through despite opposition from Jefferson and James Madison. In return for the acceptance by Jefferson and Madison of Hamilton's debt refunding bill, Hamilton agreed to the national capital being moved out of New York City and being established on the Potomac River.

In 1789, American bonds were unmarketable, by 1794, the United States had a good credit rating and its bonds were selling at a premium in Europe. Talleyrand, later the French foreign minister but then in the United States to escape the Terror, explained why. The United States bonds, he said, were "safe and free from reverses. They have been funded in such a sound manner and the prosperity of this country is growing so rapidly that there can be no doubt of their solvency." By 1801 Europeans held thirty-three million dollars' worth of American securities, and European capital was helping mightily to build the American economy.

These sound bonds were an important part of bank reserves, upon which banknotes could be issued, and they were a convenient means of transferring large sums of money.

But while Hamilton's plans for the national debt were accepted by Jefferson, Hamilton's idea for a banking system was subjected to intense opposition from Jefferson and his allies. Hamilton wanted to create a central bank, modeled after the Bank of England, to be called the Bank of the United States. The government would hold twenty percent of the shares, private investors the other eighty percent.

A central bank acts as a depository for government funds and a means of transferring them from one part of the country to another (no small consideration in Hamilton's day). It is also a source of loans to the government and to other banks, and it regulates the money supply.

Hamilton saw it as an instrument of fiscal efficiency, economic regulation, and sound money creation. Jefferson saw it as another giveaway to the rich, as he expected the bank to be very profitable. And it was, central banks always are. In 2014, the Federal Reserve made a profit of $98 billion, which went to the Treasury. Jefferson also saw it as a potential instrument of tyranny.

Furthermore, Jefferson and Madison thought it was patently unconstitutional for the federal government to establish a bank.

Hamilton did not like the idea of the government itself issuing paper money because he thought that governments could not be trusted to exert self-discipline. Allow government to print money, thought Hamilton, and it will print it to solve fiscal problems rather than using less politically palatable choices, such as raising taxes or cutting spending. Hamilton thought that an independent central bank, with its shareholders' capital at risk, could supply not only a medium of exchange but the discipline needed to keep the money sound.

These banknotes would circulate at par and relieve the desperate shortage of cash. Further, because the central bank could refuse the notes issued by state banks that got out of line—an act that would mean that no one else would take them either—it would supply discipline to the whole banking system.

Jefferson argued that because the Constitution does not specifically empower the government to charter a bank, the government could not do so. This doctrine has come to be known as strict construction.

Hamilton argued for a doctrine of implied powers. To convince President Washington to sign the bill, Hamilton wrote an essay explaining and constitutionally justifying his plan. He apparently wrote it in a single night, all 15,000 words of it—and remember that Hamilton wrote with a quill pen, not a computer. In it he argued that, if the government was to deal successfully with its enumerated powers, it must be supreme in deciding how to do so.

President Washington, his doubted quieted, signed the bill chartering the Bank of the United States for twenty years.

Again, Hamilton's plan for an American banking system worked brilliantly. There were only three state banks in 1790. By 1800 there were twenty-nine and 250 by 1811. Bank failure was extremely rare in these years.

No wonder Daniel Webster, with typical grandiloquence, would later say of Hamilton that, "The whole country perceived with delight, and the world saw with admiration. He smote the rock of the national resources, and abundant streams gushed forth. He touched the dead corpse of the public credit, and it sprung to its feet. The fabled birth of Minerva from the brain of Jove was hardly more sudden or more perfect than the financial system of the United States as it burst forth from the conception of Alexander Hamilton."

But while Jefferson had lost the battle over establishing the Bank of the United States, he won the war. In 1811, when the charter of the Bank came up for renewal, James Madison was president. Unlike Jefferson, who was an ideologue to his fingertips, Madison was capable of learning from real-world experience. And he, having seen how effective the Bank had been, now favored renewing the bank's charter. But Madison was constitutionally over-scrupulous and would not use executive pressure to get Congress to renew it. He simply submitted the bill and waited for Congress to decide. When his vice president, George Clinton, broke a tie in the Senate by voting against the bank—probably the only independent political act in vice-presidential history—the bank died.

Congress then, having destroyed the government's prime means of borrowing, soon declared war on Great Britain, the only country on earth capable of attacking the United States. It then adjourned without making any provision to pay for the war. It was probably the most feckless act in the history of the United States Congress, a title for which there is no shortage of candidates.

We very nearly lost the war by simply running out of money to pay for it, but managed to escape with a draw. Chastised, Congress chartered a Second Bank of the United States in 1816, but it never had the power the first bank had had. Banking discipline began to fray.

State banking laws varied greatly, some had good bank regulatory systems and some had very poor ones. Some, following Jefferson, kept banks small by forbidding branching. But small banks are inherently weak banks, dependent on local economies.

Andrew Jackson, a thorough-going Jeffersonian when it came to money and banking, vetoed the renewal of the Second Bank's charter in 1832. Until 1913, the United States would be the only major country in the world without a central bank. One result was the very high amplitude of the American business cycle, with bigger booms and bigger busts than in other countries.

With discipline much loosened by the decline and fall of central banking in the United States, banks, and bad banking, proliferated, as did bank failure. By 1840 there were a thousand banks in operation in the United States; twenty years later the number had nearly doubled. But almost half the banks founded between 1810 and 1820 failed before 1825. A similar percentage of those founded in the 1830s failed before 1845.

In the seventy-three years between the adoption of the Constitution and the outbreak of the Civil War, the money supply grew no less than forty times, from $15 million to $600 million. Only 25 percent of this money supply, however, was in the form of gold and silver. The rest was in demand deposits and banknotes.

With most of these thousands of banks issuing banknotes, knowing which ones were good and which were not was a huge problem, even though most only circulated locally. The notes could only be redeemed for specie—gold and silver—at the bank's head-quarters, and some banks came to be called "wildcat banks" as their headquarters were, deliberately, "out among the wildcats" and hard to find. Publishers issued what were called banknote detectors to help identify which notes were good, which dubious, and which were known to be fraudulent. It was monetary chaos.

But just like the prospect of being hanged in a fortnight, great wars concentrate minds wonderfully. And the American Civil War was the greatest war fought in the Western world in the century between the fall of Napoleon and the outbreak of World War I. The fiscal demands were enormous, with the national debt soaring from $65 million to $2.7 billion. In 1865, the United States Government became the first government in history to spend a billion dollars in a single year.

The federal government quickly began issuing fiat money, so-called greenbacks, amounting to $450 million by the war's end, about eleven percent of total federal outlays. While people were forced to accept them in payment of debt, for they were declared legal tender, the government itself would not accept them in payment of taxes, which had to be paid in gold.

But while these greenbacks, whose value in gold fluctuated with the fortunes of the Union army, caused considerable inflation, roughly seventy-five percent by the war's end, it was nowhere near as bad as in the Confederacy. With a much smaller ability to raise money through bond issues and taxes, the Confederacy was forced to issue about a billion and half dollars in fiat money to pay its bills. Southern states and cities also issued paper money, and, because the South had limited facilities for both papermaking and printing, counterfeiters had a field day.

Gresham's law, that bad money drives out good, immediately kicked in and gold and silver coins disappeared into mattresses as people spent the fiat money. And, of course, inflation took off. The South suffered an inflation of about 700 percent just in the first two years of the war. By the war's end, confederate money had become worthless and the Southern economy was in shambles. It would take a century to recover.

To help finance the war, Congress also finally tackled the chaotic American banking system. In 1863, it established a system of nationally chartered banks. These banks had to have at least $50,000 in capital, a large sum at the time, and had to hold sixty percent of that capital in United States Treasury securities. National banks were subject to rigorous oversight by the new comptroller of the currency, by such means as sudden, unannounced audits. These banks were allowed to issue banknotes, but only using a uniform design, supplied by the government and the notes had to be backed, 100 percent, by pledged Treasury bonds.

The federal government thought that most state banks would take national charters, but they didn't, as many could not meet the capital requirements. By the end of 1863, there were 134 national banks, almost all of them new banks. Changes in the law in 1864 sped conversions but still, most banks remained state-chartered.

So in March 1865, Congress imposed a ten-percent tax on the face value of state-bank issued banknotes, driving those banks out of the banknote business. It also caused many of them to take national charters. By 1866, there were 1600 national banks and only about 200 state banks still in existence. There were also, of course, mutual savings banks, private banks, savings and loan associations, and credit unions. None of them issued banknotes, but all acted as banks, taking deposits and making loans and each type was regulated separately. This multiplicity of bank regulation, unknown in any other country, would be the source of disaster in the 20th century more than once.

Because of the Jeffersonian hatred for big banks, national banks were forbidden, until 1922, to have branches or operate across state lines, so their number grew quickly as the country's economy and population exploded in size after the Civil War. Meanwhile state banks discovered that, while they could no longer print banknotes, they could still create money by simply crediting a borrower's balance in a checking account. Their number also began to grow quickly. By 1900 there were 3,731 national banks and 4,405 state banks. By 1920 there were about 30,000 banks in the United States, almost all of them single, unit banks, dependant of the prosperity of just the local community.

But at least the era of wildcat banking was at an end. By the end of the Civil War there were only three types of paper money in the country, national bank banknotes, backed by bank reserves, United States Notes, the old greenbacks, redeemable in gold beginning in 1879, and silver certificates that could be redeemed in silver.

The country was back on the gold standard.

The gold standard simply means that a country establishes the value of its currency in gold and stands ready to buy or sell unlimited quantities of it at that price. In the early 18th century the value of the British pound had been set at 3 pounds, 17 shillings, ten and a half pence per troy ounce of gold by Sir Isaac Newton, of all people, enjoying the perks of a largely no-show—but well remunerated—job as Master of the King's Mint. In 1821, after the Napoleonic Wars, the Bank of England went on the gold standard. Many other major countries followed. The value of the dollar was set at $20.66 per ounce of gold.

While the gold standard was popular with the wealthy, especially in the industrialized northeast, for it effectively makes inflation impossible and facilitates overseas trade, the less affluent hated it. Most Americans in the late 19th century were still farmers and most farmers are chronic debtors. Like all debtors they liked inflation as it made it possible to pay back their debts in cheaper money.

Faced with a strong demand by one influential group—bankers and industrialists—for a gold standard, and an equally strong demand for an inflationary monetary policy by another influential group, farmers, the government, as so often happens in a democracy, tried to have it both ways.

For a while, it even worked.

While returning to the gold standard, Congress passed the Bland-Allison Act in 1878, requiring the Treasury to buy between $2 and $4 million in silver every month and turn it into coin or silver certificates at the ratio of 16-to-1. In other words sixteen ounces of silver was declared by Congressional fiat to be worth one ounce of gold.

At the time, that was about the market price. But as ever more silver poured out of western mines—in the 1880s Nevada and Colorado alone accounted for fully forty percent of world silver production—the price declined to about 20-to-1 by 1890. That year Congress ordered the Treasury to buy 4.5 million ounces of silver a month and turn it into coin or silver certificates at the 16-to-1 ratio, a sure recipe for inflation.

With its silver policy greatly increasing the money supply, and the gold standard keeping the value of the dollar steady, the government managed, in effect, both to guarantee and to forbid inflation.

As anyone who has taken an introductory economics course could predict, Gresham's law kicked in again. Silver, worth one-twentieth the price of gold in the market, was declared to be worth one-sixteenth the price of gold when coined as money. So, naturally, people began to spend the silver and hoard the gold, and gold started trickling out of the Treasury.

With the major depression that began in 1893, that trickle turned into a flood. Soon the Treasury's gold supply was getting dangerously low and Congress refused to authorize another bond issue to replenish it.

J. P. Morgan, thoroughly alarmed, took the train to Washington to see President Cleveland. But the President refused to see him, knowing that "Wall Street," then as now, was the left's favorite whipping boy, and J. P. Morgan was the very embodiment of Wall Street.

"I have come down to see the president," Morgan said in his best imperial manner, "and I am going to stay until I see him."

With the situation rapidly deteriorating, Cleveland saw him the next morning. Morgan's lawyers had dug up an obscure Civil-War-era law allowing the government to issue bonds to buy coin without congressional authorization. Morgan offered that he and August Belmont, Jr., who represented the Rothschilds, would buy $100 million in gold in Europe and give it to the Treasury in exchange for the new bonds. Further he promised to keep the market steady and prevent the gold from leaching out of the Treasury once again.

He was, in effect, offering to act as a central bank, insulating the Treasury from market forces. It worked.

The next year the depression began to lift but William Jennings Bryan swept to the presidential nomination of the Democratic Party by promising to prevent mankind from being crucified upon a cross of gold. He lost the election badly to William McKinley whose slogan was "Sound Money, protection, and prosperity."

In 1907 Morgan again acted as a central bank to deal with the financial panic of that year, and people began to realize that a central bank was now a necessity. After all, J. P. Morgan, over seventy at that point, would not be around forever.

In 1913, ironically the year that Morgan died, the Federal Reserve System was created. But while Wall Street had wanted a single bank, located in New York, twelve banks were created in cities across the country. Again, the Jeffersonian dread of powerful banks was at work.

In a banking panic, member banks could maintain liquidity by borrowing from the Federal Reserve as a lender of last resort using their loan portfolios as security. National banks were required to join and so could state banks that could meet the requirements. But most could not meet them. Thus the very banks that most needed the ability to borrow from the Federal Reserve in an emergency couldn't do so.

As rural areas of the country began to go into recession in the middle of the 1920s, thanks to falling food prices, the banks that served small-town America began to fail. By the late 1920s these failures were averaging about 500 a year.

But when the Great Depression began in 1929, the number of bank failures exploded while the money supply contracted sharply. There was about a one-third deflation between 1929 and 1933, greatly exacerbating the Depression. By the fall of 1932, bank runs, where panicked depositors suddenly withdraw their funds, fearing failure and thus making that failure a self-fulfilling prophecy, began to spread from individual banks to the banking system as a whole.

By the time Franklin Roosevelt was inaugurated on March 4, 1933, state governors had closed banks in 38 states, and the other ten had limited withdrawals. The American banking system, and thus its money supply, was near death.

Roosevelt closed all the banks and gave his first fireside chat, explaining what the government had done and assuring the public that when a bank reopened it was because the government had found it to be sound and therefore it was a safer place for one's money than the mattress.

The public believed him and money began to flow once more into banks. It had been a near-run thing.

The Federal Reserve was reorganized, deposit insurance ended bank runs, and Federal-Reserve-issued banknotes became the dominant form of paper money. Gold coins were withdrawn from circulation and it became illegal to hold the metal in bullion form. The system steadied.

In 1951 a man named William Boyle, who worked for the Franklin National Bank in Long Island, invented the credit card, an idea that quickly spread, creating the first new form of money since the banknote.

In the 1960s, the price of silver rising, the United States stopped minting silver coins, making so-called sandwich coins instead. Thus, technically, they were not coins at all, but tokens. Nevertheless, now a trivial portion of the money supply, they continued to be accepted and were therefore, if not coins, still money. Gresham's law kicked in, however, and the old silver coins quickly disappeared from circulation.

In 1971, President Nixon severed the last link between American money and precious metals when he no longer allowed foreign central banks to redeem dollars for gold. The United States now had nothing but fiat money.

So why didn't it inflate into worthlessness as fiat money had so often done in the past? One reason was that most of the money supply was now in the form of demand deposits, not notes or coin. Money had largely become electronic blips in the bowels of vast and interconnected computer systems.

The second was that an international currency market had sprung up, trading trillions of dollars in currencies a day. If the market thought a country was pursuing unwise monetary policies, it could devalue that country's currency with startling speed. France found that out in 1980, when newly-elected President François Mitterrand nationalized the French banking system and tried to move the country toward socialism. The rapidly sinking value of the franc forced him into a hasty retreat.

Today, coins are surely on the way to extinction after 2700 years. It now costs the government two cents to mint a penny, most of which end up in coffee cans in bedroom closets. And banknotes are quickly declining as plastic becomes ubiquitous. Even prostitutes, I'm reliably informed, now happily accept plastic in payment for their services.

The Internal Revenue Service would, of course, love to eliminate cash altogether to prevent tax cheating. Drug dealers and waiters are less enthusiastic about that prospect.

Soon, I'm sure, one won't even have to use plastic. As you make your way through a check-out line, the iPhone in your pocket will sync to the store computer, download a receipt, and you're on your way.

It will, indeed, be a brave new world, one Thomas Jefferson could not have dreamed of and would, surely, have hated. I doubt Alexander Hamilton could have conceived of it either, but I bet he would love it.

PETER SCHIFF

How to Think About the Federal Reserve

Most of the economic problems that we have today can be laid at the foot of the Federal Reserve, also known as the Fed. It is certainly responsible for the degradation of the American economy, which is in large part due to the artificially low interest rates that have prevailed for most of the last twenty years. Artificially fixing the cost of credit has had disastrous consequences for the American economy.

The Fed's actions have discouraged capital investment, savings, and production. Conversely, it has encouraged reckless consumption and speculation. All of this has helped transform America from an industrial powerhouse into the world's largest debtor nation. We buy things that are made in other countries and borrow the money to do it. The Fed has succeeded in replacing the American economy with a gigantic bubble. True, it has helped to elevate the stock market, the bond market, the real estate market, rare art, and collectible automobiles, as asset prices have risen significantly. But at the same time, the Fed has been the principal architect of a widening divide between the very rich and everybody else. Members of what used to be the middle and lower classes are angry and frustrated, not realizing that the Fed is mostly to blame for this state of affairs.

The Federal Reserve has been the main barrier to economic growth. The federal government has been complicit, of course, but if it wasn't for the Fed being willing to accommodate government spending by monetizing it, and by keeping interest rates artificially low, the government would have had to come to terms with its insolvency years ago—it would have been forced to cut spending. So if one is upset about the growth of government, he should look no further than the Fed, which is enabling it. The Fed pretends it doesn't have a choice, that it must accommodate bigger government, but that's not true. It is supposed to be independent, but instead it acts like an arm of the federal government whose job is to facilitate government spending and deficits. Its actions have enabled deficits to grow to unprecedented levels.

When it was created in 1913, the Federal Reserve was not allowed to buy U.S. government debt. That was not part of its original mission, and it likely would not have been created had its founders known it was going to be an engine of inflation. But once America entered World War I, the Federal Reserve Act was amended in such a way as to enable the Fed to buy U.S. treasuries, so the government could finance the war more efficiently. This change, which was meant as a temporary measure to help win the war, became permanent.

When Congress passed this amendment, it was worried about the problem of too much debt, so it also instituted a debt ceiling. Unfortunately, that ceiling has been raised every time it has been approached, until just recently when it was suspended altogether. The government could never have grown to the size it is today if it had to pay for its activities with real money. If it had to tax American citizens to pay for the spending, those citizens would certainly have objected. Today's government is able to promise something for nothing, all because of the Fed.

The United States today is on the verge of the biggest economic catastrophe in its history. The 2008 financial crisis was bad, but it was nothing compared to what's coming. What the Federal

Reserve did in the aftermath of the 2008 crisis made all the problems that caused the crisis even worse. What is going to exacerbate the next crisis is that fact that the Fed still doesn't understand its role in causing that problem.

Not only does the Fed not understand how its policies caused the 2008 financial crisis, it still doesn't understand what caused the Great Depression. In the latter half of the 1920s, the Fed kept interest rates too low, which it did deliberately. The Fed's goal was to try to prop up the British pound, so it lowered interest rates in the United States. This led to speculative bubbles in the stock market and in the real estate market. Eventually the Fed raised interest rates and the bubble popped in 1929.

This by itself would not have caused the Great Depression. However, President Herbert Hoover decided against a market-based approach in addressing the problem, which had been the norm in the past. Previously, in tough times, the government did what everybody else did and tightened its belt. If the economy was weak, the government cut spending in order to be less of a burden on a weak economy. Instead, Hoover became the first president to try a fiscal stimulus. The result of his attempt to prop up the economy was a depression, which, after FDR radically expanded Hoover's efforts in the form of the New Deal, became the Great Depression.

Today's Fed looks at the Great Depression and thinks the mistake wasn't lowering interest rates, rather, the mistake was that rates were raised in the first place. The Fed thinks that the solution to problems brought about by interest rates being too low and government spending too much is to make interest rates even lower and for the government to spend even more money. The Fed is in a big ditch and thinks the way out is to keep digging.

During the 2008 crisis, the Federal Reserve bailed everybody out and postponed a lot of the financial pain, because a lot of the bad debt that was owned by the private sector was bought by the government. Unfortunately, the government's liabilities have skyrocketed, and the next crisis is going to be a crisis at the sovereign level. The U.S. government, eventually, is going to experience a crisis in the dollar and in the bond market. Investors are going to lose confidence in the value of the dollar and in the U.S. government's ability to pay its debts.

I should add that the problem goes far beyond an $18.5 trillion national debt. Including the unfunded, off-budget liabilities that are not part of the Treasury, America's debt is closer to $100 trillion. If interest rates were allowed to rise, the U.S. government couldn't afford to service its debt, let alone retire it.

The Federal Reserve wants to claim credit for fixing the American economy. Yet, since the Fed embarked on its current program, the economy has only gotten worse. Real wages have fallen. Millions of people have left the labor force and are no longer working.

Consider home ownership, which is at its lowest level in 50 years. Many people today are renting, and rents are rising rapidly, despite the fact that interest rates are at zero and someone can buy a house with three and a half percent down. Even though the loan would be guaranteed by the government, Americans are still too broke to qualify. What would happen to the housing market if interest rates went up? Do you recall all those banks that were too big to fail and were bailed out? They're a lot bigger now. All of them would fail if the Fed were to raise interest rates by any significant amount. The Fed talks a lot about raising interest rates, but it knows that it can't. It can't admit this fact because if it does, then the party is over. It would be an admission of failure. When the Fed first announced its quantitative easing program, it said it would be temporary. But that kind of program is a monetary roach motel. You can check in, but you can never check out.

Where can the Fed go from here? Either it will never raise interest rates, and the market will eventually respond to that fact, or it will raise rates. Even if it is a small increase at first the dollar is going to start to fall, and as it starts to come down, it will force commodity prices up. As a result, the Consumer Price Index is going to begin to rise above the Fed's two percent level, at which point it has said it will raise interest rates.

But I don't think the Federal Reserve will do this, because

America has too much debt. It would bankrupt all the "too-big-to-fail" financial entities. Rather than raise rates, the Fed will rationalize the inflation by saying it's transient or that it's good for us. But the Fed's failure to raise rates and to deal with inflation will put even more downward pressure on the dollar and accelerate the entire process.

If the Fed does raise rates, bond prices will fall. Foreign central banks that have invested in U.S. Treasuries will sell them and reap huge profits. They aren't stupid: they know that it's a gigantic Ponzi scheme, and that the government can never pay back any of that money. The only way to get out is to sell. Foreign central banks are going to let the dollar fall, and it will fall even more quickly than before, which will in time produce inflation in consumer prices.

Some argue we haven't had any inflation, but the people who say that don't understand what inflation is. We've had plenty of inflation, by which I mean the expansion of the money supply. The money supply has been inflated, and prices have risen as a result. Why has the stock market risen in value? Is it because corporations are earning more money? No. Is it because the plant equipment is more valuable? No. In fact, U.S. plant equipment is the oldest it's been in over 60 years. We've neglected our plant equipment. The value of real assets is going down, even as stock prices are going up. Inflation is causing that.

Despite the weak economy today, prices are rising because of the Fed's policies. During the Great Depression, prices went down by 30 percent. Imagine how much worse the Depression would have been if prices went up. This is basic economics: in order to increase demand, lower prices. The most basic concept of economics is the law of supply and demand. That is, the lower the price, the greater the demand. But the Federal Reserve thinks it's the other way around, that high prices create demand. On the contrary, low prices create demand. In today's situation of low demand, prices need to come down, and then people will be able to afford to buy things.

So why aren't prices falling? Inflation. The government, by which I mean the Federal Reserve, is robbing consumers of the benefit of lower prices. That's inflation. One of the reasons we are not experiencing runaway inflation is because a lot of that money is offshore and owned by foreign central banks. What do these banks buy with their excess dollars? They buy bonds, which is why bond prices are stratospheric. How does this work? The Fed prints money, and we use it to buy products produced in factories. It doesn't take any effort on our part to print up money, but it took a lot of effort to manufacture a consumer good. America has a $500-billion-a-year trade deficit, which keeps prices down, because we get to export our inflation. Inflation is America's biggest export, and we import real things.

But when our international creditors lose confidence in the dollar, they're not going to want them in exchange for their products. That will mean that the inflation we create stays here. If Americans can't use their dollars to buy foreign products, there will be nothing to buy, since we don't make many of these products in America.

In theory, tariffs could work to counteract this, if there is an industry to protect. But once the industry is gone, what good are the tariffs going to do? They will lead to higher prices because there is no American substitute. Without a factory or the labor force that knows how to operate the machines, we can't make these products here. Seventy percent of GDP is people spending money, i.e., shopping. What is the economic output of spending money? Nothing. Output is the products you produce, not consuming what has already been produced. That means Americans are financing economic growth that takes place outside the United States. When foreigners lose confidence in the dollar, the dollar's going to collapse, and all that exported inflation is going to come back home. By the time that inflation tsunami washes back up on our shores, it will be too late to do anything about it.

The Federal Reserve has reached the false conclusion that it can print money with no negative consequences. Yet, the results of this disastrous policy can be seen in the real economy, where the average American is suffering a decline in his standard of living. Rather than adopt policies that encourage the savings and investment necessary for legitimate economic growth, the Fed has substituted a bubble economy, as it tries to convince Americans to take on more debt and buy more stuff.

The Fed's easy money approach will lead to another economic crisis unless the United States eventually rights the ship and comes to terms with its debt. But so far there is no political will in Congress, the White House, or the Fed to do anything about the problem. The path that we're on can only lead to a currency crisis.

In the 2008 crisis, nobody lost any money. The government bailed everyone out. But if the Fed ever has to raise interest rates to defend the dollar, nobody will get a bailout. If the Fed is raising rates, selling Treasuries, and shrinking its balance sheet, nobody will get bailed out. Not only will the bondholders lose money, depositors will also lose money, because the Federal Deposit Insurance Corporation (FDIC) has no money of its own.

In fact, if the Fed has to raise interest rates to fight inflation, the U.S. government will have to default on its Treasury bonds. There won't be any money to pay the interest. Did you know one third of the U.S. Treasury bond market matures in the next year? What happens if our creditors want their money back? We don't have it. The government counts on everybody rolling the debt over to the next year.

If the Fed raises interest rates, and the U.S. Treasury has to default, people that have bank accounts are going to lose their money. The government is going to have to come clean with all of those Americans to whom it has promised money. It will have to tell them that even though they were promised a lot of money in exchange for their votes, that money is gone, the government is broke, and they won't be receiving what they were promised. That's what would happen if the Fed did the right thing and raised interest rates to stop the dollar from becoming worthless. The government is going to have to be honest about the financial situation and its inability to keep its promises. If it doesn't do that then we're going to have a complete collapse of the dollar.

There is no easy way out. When someone borrows beyond his capacity to repay, his debts aren't paid. In this case, the Fed can be honest about it, and default, or it can be dishonest, and inflate. Either way the consequences are the same: The creditor receives his money but it isn't worth much, or he receives less money.

I think our creditors would be better off if they took a haircut. If there was a legitimate restructuring of the debt and the government paid out 30 cents on the dollar to its creditors—not only bondholders, but Social Security recipients and other participants in government wealth transfer programs—or applied means- or asset-testing to all government programs, then everyone would be much better off. On the other hand, if politicians try to pay everybody off using a printing press, the real loss in purchasing power will be much greater. You might receive 100 cents on the dollar, but that 100 cents might be worth only two cents, a much bigger haircut than would be the case if the government were to be honest.

America became the wealthiest country in the history of the world without a central bank, which was not created until 1913. But as the Fed has grown and government has grown along with it, our wealth has diminished dramatically. We're no longer the world's wealthiest economy, we're the world's biggest debtor. In 2008, the government ran a successful propaganda campaign—it blamed the financial crisis on capitalism. It said the crisis resulted from a lack of regulation, from capitalism run amok, from too much greed. The solution, we were told, was more government. The Federal Reserve was given more power, even though it created the crisis. Government today tends to infiltrate the free market, screw it up, and blame the result on the free market. This, we are told, is why we need even more government.

It is my hope that in this next crisis, Americans will understand the root cause of it, and will demand a return to sound money and limited government. The good news is that capitalism works. Imagine how much more rapidly we could raise the standard of living for all Americans if the government would simply get out of the way.

WILLIAM WALTON

The Problem of Crony Capitalism Today

I used to think that the problem of crony capitalism was not a simple story of good versus evil—of greedy capitalists, intrusive and coercive regulators, venal politicians, and K-Street lobbyists versus the rest of us. But after digging more deeply into this issue, I have concluded that it is that simple after all. We have a massive and growing problem in America: It's a moral issue, it explains why economic growth is anemic, and it's bipartisan.

The problem is that the size and scope of the federal government is so large that it's impossible to know where business starts and government ends. The federal budget has ballooned to $4 trillion. Federal regulatory compliance costs add up to another $1.7 trillion and affect every industry. 87,000 new federal rules have been issued since 1993. What all this means is that business has a lot at stake in Washington.

Businesses complain that regulations are intrusive and coercive, but when they lobby for maintaining and increasing subsidies and mandates at the expense of taxpayers and consumers, they threaten public support for business and free markets. The growing and incestuous relationship between business and government in America is a destructive force, undermining not just our economy and our political system, but the foundations of our culture. This kind of collusion between business and government used to be known as rent-seeking, but today we call it cronyism.

Regulation combined with an incredibly complex tax code are big drags on business and economic growth. They are also the primary means to suppress competition and keep new entrants out of the marketplace. At the risk of gross oversimplification, there are essentially two ways for a business to make money: The first is by competing for customers in a free market system of voluntary exchange. The second is by petitioning government for special privileges such as subsidies for sugar and other farm crops, or mandates for products like ethanol. Other special privileges include grants, loans, tax credits, favorable regulations, bailouts, loan guarantees, targeted tax breaks, and no-bid contracts. Government can also grant monopoly status, erect barriers to entry, and provide protection from foreign competition. Less obvious, but also a form of cronyism, are occupational licenses such as teacher certifications and school accreditations.

The first way is the right way. It has the twin virtues of being both moral and promoting economic growth and well-being. The right way is people engaging in what economists call "voluntary exchanges" that improve lives and make the economy grow. It is the process that has allowed us to live in a time where there's been more improvement in the human condition in the past hundred years than in all the previous centuries combined. Every measure of material human welfare—such as health, wealth, nutrition, education, transportation, communications, and leisure time—has shown amazing gains. And virtually all of this innovation has been created and driven by entrepreneurs competing in a free market of voluntary exchange.

In contrast to coercion and cronyism, voluntary exchange is the process whereby people willingly trade one item for another, making both parties to the transaction better off as a result. This principle applies to the non-profit world as well. When a donor voluntarily writes a check for a charitable cause, both parties benefit. The donor is able to give to a cause that matters to him, and the recipient has more resources to do its work.

Voluntary exchange lies at the heart of free enterprise, market efficiency, and entrepreneurship. The network of relationships that emerges or evolves out of this trading process is called "the market." Millions of voluntary exchanges every day make the world better off. They have the great virtue of being both moral and promoting economic growth.

By contrast, government taxes and regulations mandate involuntary exchanges, which rely on coercion. For example, try not paying your taxes, and see who shows up to seize your assets or put you in jail.

It is voluntary exchange that is most under threat from the government and its crony partners. Whether it's the minimum wage, EPA regulations, abortion insurance mandates, or small business licensing, our entrepreneurial freedoms are being eroded. Increasingly we are being told, for example, what we can sell, to whom we can sell it, and what wages and benefits we must provide. This kind of approach stifles entrepreneurship, innovation, economic freedom, and growth. It also aids and abets entrenched political and economic incumbents.

Now, I don't believe that American politicians, bureaucrats, and businesses today are more venal or dishonest than those of the past. There has always been cronyism and people seeking special favors from the government. What's changed is that the scope and reach of the federal government has expanded dramatically.

Before the 1930s, the general consensus in America—confirmed by the Supreme Court—was that the Constitution severely restricted the power of the federal government. Then a constitutional revolution occurred beginning in 1937 that dramatically expanded government power. The Supreme Court issued a series of rulings that changed everything.

One allowed Congress to delegate its powers to federal agencies. Another gutted the Commerce Clause, giving the federal government regulatory power over virtually all manufacturing and agriculture in the United States. A third declared Social Security constitutional, while at the same time reinterpreting the General Welfare Clause to allow Congress to spend money on virtually anything.

Fast forward to today. There is little chance that these rulings can be reversed. As Charles Murray observed, "To reverse any of these rulings would mean that about 90% of everything the federal government does is unconstitutional. That's not going to happen."

Before the New Deal in the 1930s, very few industries were affected by what went on in Washington. Only those who ran a railroad or a utility, or who were looking for tariff protection from foreign competition, had to think about dealing with the federal government. The New Deal ushered in the Civil Aeronautics Board, the FCC, and about a dozen other industry-specific agencies. Despite these developments, only a small number of industries were affected. As late as 1960, only a handful of corporations had even a small office in Washington.

Then came Lyndon Johnson's Great Society and a great outpouring of regulations from Washington. Almost 30,000 pages were added to the Code of Federal Regulations by the end of the 1960s. The Civil Rights Act of 1964 brought about unprecedented federal oversight of employee hiring, firing, and promotion. Richard Nixon later confirmed and expanded this new regulatory state. From 1970 to 1974, 16 new major regulatory agencies were established, including the EPA and OSHA, and the powers of the EEOC were expanded. What made these regulatory agencies different was the fact that they were given economy-wide authority to regulate every business in the country. By 2012, the number of pages in the Federal Code of Regulations had risen to nearly 175,000. And on a parallel path, the federal tax code became increasingly complex and massively intrusive, with thousands of deductions, incentives, penalties, and special favors for virtually every industry in America. As a result, we now have a tax code that is four million words long.

How did businesses respond? They went to Washington. By the end of the 1970s, most major corporations and trade groups had offices in Washington.

As the regulatory state has grown, the job of politicians has changed, and they now serve as liaisons with regulatory agencies, in addition to their constitutional function as legislators. Politicians now have enormous power over the activities of the private sector, and billions of dollars are often at stake when a bill is under consideration by Congress. This is the principal cause for the flow of lobbying money to K Street. As Charles Murray puts it, "Corruption in the political process varies directly with the number and value of things that politicians have to sell." That value has increased exponentially. Politics has now become a way to get rich.

It's a seldom-remarked fact of American politics that the people in the top leadership positions, including senators, cabinet officers, governors, ranking members of the House of Representatives—Democrats and Republicans alike—live a life utterly removed from that of the people they rule. The trappings of office include cars and drivers, private jets, four-star restaurants, and skyboxes, all of which they receive for free. They aren't carrying their own luggage. Most come to Washington filled with ideals and plans for change. Then, the system corrupts them. As Al Regnery, former publisher of *The American Spectator*, once said: "They come to clean up the cesspool in Washington, then they discover it's a hot tub."

A few years ago, I had my first direct experience with the lobbying culture of Washington. I learned that even politicians I believe are among the good guys can get captured by the way Congress and the special interests work today.

As a CEO of a highly regulated financial company, I concluded, like many other CEOs, that I needed to understand how the political process worked, if nothing else to protect our company's interests from harmful regulation and legislation. So we set up a political action committee (PAC). Then I was invited to a weekend-long PAC event sponsored by a senator whom I still have great respect for. It was held at a NASCAR race in Homestead, Florida. At the time, a transportation bill was in the works. It was a huge bill, and most of it wasn't about transportation. There were about 30–40 attendees, mostly lobbyists, as it turned out. As the weekend progressed, my senator friend looked at me quizzically from time to time as if I was going to bring something up. Finally, as we were leaving on Sunday, he asked me why I was there. I told him I wanted good judges, less regulation, and tax reform. He looked at me, smiled, and said, "You're new to Washington aren't you? Everybody here has got something in the transportation bill."

It seems like every time Congress passes a big new bill, it intentionally or unintentionally ends up benefiting incumbents, big business, and entrenched interests, while at the same time hurting small business and consumers. Two recent examples spring to mind: Sarbanes-Oxley and Dodd Frank.

Dodd-Frank was supposedly aimed at Wall Street, but it hit Main Street much harder. Community-based financial institutions, which make the bulk of small business loans, have been overwhelmed by the law's complexity. Government figures indicate that the United States is losing on average one community bank or credit union per day. About 100 new banks were started every year between 1990 and the financial crisis in 2008. From 2009 through 2013, only about seven new banks were formed, an astounding decline.

There are several reasons for the decline in the number of small banks:

- Increasing regulatory compliance costs. For example, United Southern Bank in Kentucky is about the same size as it was in 2009 but has had to add 15 employees to ensure compliance with new federal regulations.
- The Federal Reserve is manipulating the money supply to keep interest rates near zero, which helps big banks but crushes small bank interest rate margins.
- It takes over 24 million man-hours per year to comply with the rules imposed by Dodd-Frank. By contrast, it only took 20 million man-hours to build the Panama Canal.

Goldman Sachs CEO Lloyd Blankfein has said—quite revealingly—that Goldman is a big beneficiary of Dodd-Frank's more intense regulatory requirements, which have, as he said, "raised the barriers to entry into the banking business higher than at any other time in modern history." JP Morgan CEO Jamie Dimon essentially said the same thing, when he explained, using one of Warren Buffet's favorite terms, that Dodd-Frank helped create a "bigger economic moat" around the megabanks. As Tim Carney of the *Washington Times* has written, "Regulations like Dodd-Frank protect the giants because politics and lobbying are home games for the big guys. Goldman is famously close with Washington, and the revolving door between Goldman and its regulators is well-trafficked."

More regulation increases the value of lobbyists and lawyers, particularly those who used to be lawmakers and regulators. Wauwatosa Community Bank can't afford to hire many former members of the House Financial Services Committee.

This is a big problem.

Community banks represent the vast majority of U.S. banks. They are critical to the economy because they are more likely to make small-business loans. Community banks hold 46% of loans to farms and small businesses but hold only 14% of total banking industry assets. For rural communities, small banks are often the only lender, since the big banks are closing branches.

What about Sarbanes-Oxley? For decades, U.S. stock exchanges were seen by companies around the world as the most prestigious location to list shares. But the number of public listings in the U.S. peaked at 8,884 companies in 1997. It's now down to about 5,000. Regulations such as the Sarbanes-Oxley Act have had a chilling effect on companies wishing to go public in the U.S., but very little effect on established companies.

For example, regulatory costs are estimated at $4 million annually for an emerging growth company when it goes public, which often means the loss of most of its profits. At the same time, emerging markets such as China have lured more companies to their exchanges. Between 2000 and 2012, the U.S. averaged just 177 listings annually. Meanwhile, the number of listings on exchanges in China nearly tripled to more than 4,000.

Why does this matter? Emerging public growth companies create the most jobs. A recent study showed that these so-called "gazelles" created as much as 75% of the high-paying jobs in America. Now CEOs and venture capital backers of emerging growth companies don't want the hassles and costs of running a public company. So instead they choose to be acquired. The problem is that big companies don't create jobs. Their acquisition strategy is often to buy an emerging growth company for its technology, then fire the people.

Let's return to the problem of cronyism. Lobbying has evolved from companies protecting themselves from such things as tax increases and regulations to using the political process to help them become more profitable. The classic case is the Medicare Modernization Act of 2003 which ushered in Medicare Part B drug benefits. It's estimated that pharmaceutical companies spent about $130 million to help get the law passed, while the payoff has been estimated to be over $200 billion in new drug sales over a ten-year period, all of it paid for by taxpayers.

Another example is the ethanol mandate, which is among the least defensible corporate-welfare boondoggles Washington has ever created. It forces drivers to put corn alcohol in their cars by forcing refiners to blend it with real gasoline. Yet, ethanol is far less efficient than gasoline. It increases food prices by taking up cropland that could be used for other crops. It makes animal feed more expensive, hurting ranchers and boosting meat prices. It places extraordinary stress on water supplies.

Or consider the case of General Electric, which in last year's annual report described itself as "A New Kind of Industrial Company." In the last decade, GE spent over $300 million on lobbying. CEO Jeffrey Immelt has visited the Obama White House 33 times. Why would a business spend this kind of time and money lobbying? Because it produces results: General Electric paid no federal income taxes from 2008 to 2012. Instead it received $3.1 billion in refunds on $27.5 billion in profits during this period. It's received over $2 billion in federal loan guarantees for wind and solar projects. It was a big recipient of money from the Troubled Asset Relief Program or TARP, which was meant to bail out banks. But GE Capital is not a bank. It received subsidies of $132 million for a lithium battery company that subsequently went bankrupt.

Of course, one of the most effective ways to lobby is to wrap your special interest in a cloak of public good. In the name of protecting the environment, GE was one of the principal advocates of energy legislation that effectively outlawed incandescent light bulbs and replaced them with LED bulbs. This allowed GE to get out of the unprofitable and low margin incandescent light bulb business and into the much more profitable and high margin LED business. Prior to the legislation, consumers balked at paying the higher LED prices, but now we are forced to pony up.

Perhaps it's no surprise, given all of this, that GE CEO Immelt appeared on the Charlie Rose show and praised the Communist government of China: "State run Communists may not be your cup of tea—but their government works." He also told his company's shareholders that "in a reset economy, the government will be a regulator; and also an industry policy champion, a financier, and a key partner. The interaction between government and business will change forever." Yes, GE *is* a new kind of industrial company.

Are there any solutions to the pervasive and growing problem of cronyism? If so, they need to be big and radical ones. Tinkering around the edges with such things as term limits or campaign finance reform is not likely to change much in Washington so long as trillions of dollars are at stake.

One place I would start is getting rid of the income tax code, and replacing it with the flat tax or a fair tax. This would eliminate tax code cronyism and ignite the economy.

Whatever we do, we need to think big and act now.

LUDWIG VON MISES

From "The Functions of Money" in
The Theory of Money and Credit

The Functions of Money

The General Economic Conditions for the Use of Money

Where the free exchange of goods and services is unknown, money is not wanted. In a state of society in which the division of labor was a purely domestic matter and production and consumption were consummated within the single household it would be just as useless as it would be for an isolated man. But even in an economic order based on division of labor, money would still be unnecessary if the means of production were socialized, the control of production and the distribution of the finished product were in the hands of a central body, and individuals were not allowed to exchange the consumption goods allotted to them for the consumption goods allotted to others.

Ludwig von Mises, "The Functions of Money," in *The Theory of Money and Credit* (New Haven: Yale University Press, 1953), 29–37. See also the Ludwig von Mises Institute—https://mises.org/library/theory-money-and-credit.

The phenomenon of money presupposes an economic order in which production is based on division of labor and in which private property consists not only in goods of the first order (consumption goods), but also in goods of higher orders (production goods). In such a society, there is no systematic centralized control of production, for this is inconceivable without centralized disposal over the means of production. Production is "anarchistic." What is to be produced, and how it is to be produced, is decided in the first place by the owners of the means of production, who produce, however, not only for their own needs, but also for the needs of others, and in their valuations take into account, not only the use-value that they themselves attach to their products, but also the use-value that these possess in the estimation of the other members of the community. The balancing of production and consumption takes place in the market, where the different producers meet to exchange goods and services by bargaining together. The function of money is to facilitate the business of the market by acting as a common medium of exchange.

The Origin of Money

Indirect exchange is distinguished from direct exchange according as a medium is involved or not.

Suppose that A and B exchange with each other a number of units of the commodities m and n. A acquires the commodity n because of the use-value that it has for him. He intends to consume it. The same is true of B, who acquires the commodity m for his immediate use. This is a case of direct exchange.

If there are more than two individuals and more than two kinds of commodity in the market, indirect exchange also is possible. A may then acquire a commodity p, not because he desires to consume it, but in order to exchange it for a second commodity q which he does desire to consume. Let us suppose that A brings to the market two units of the commodity m, B two units of the commodity n, and C two units of the commodity o, and that A wishes to acquire one unit of each of the commodities n and o, B one unit of each of the commodities o and m, and C one unit of each of the commodities m and n. Even in this case a direct exchange is possible if the subjective valuations of the three commodities permit the exchange of each unit of m, n, and o for a unit of one of the others. But if this or a similar hypothesis does not hold good, and in by far the greater number of all exchange transactions it does not hold good, then indirect exchange becomes necessary, and the demand for goods for immediate wants is supplemented by a demand for goods to be exchanged for others.[1]

Let us take, for example, the simple case in which the commodity p is desired only by the holders of the commodity q, while the comodity q is not desired by the holders of the commodity p but by those, say, of a third commodity r, which in its turn is desired only by the possessors of p. No direct exchange between these persons can possibly take place. If exchanges occur at all, they must be indirect; as, for instance, if the possessors of the commodity p exchange it for the commodity q and then exchange this for the commodity r which is the one they desire for their own consumption. The case is not essentially different when supply and demand do not coincide quantitatively; for example, when one indivisible good has to be exchanged for various goods in the possession of several persons.

Indirect exchange becomes more necessary as division of labor increases and wants become more refined. In the present stage of economic development, the occasions when direct exchange is both possible and actually effected have already become very exceptional. Nevertheless, even nowadays, they sometimes arise. Take, for instance, the payment of wages in kind, which is a case of direct exchange so long on the one hand as the employer uses the labor for the immediate satisfaction of his own needs and does not have to procure through exchange the goods in which the wages are paid, and so long on the other hand as the employee consumes the goods he receives and does not sell them. Such payment of wages in kind

---

1   See Wicksell, *Über Wert, Kapital und Rente* (Jena, 1893; London, 1933), pp. 50 f.

is still widely prevalent in agriculture, although even in this sphere its importance is being continually diminished by the extension of capitalistic methods of management and the development of division of labor.[2]

Thus along with the demand in a market for goods for direct consumption there is a demand for goods that the purchaser does not wish to consume but to dispose of by further exchange. It is clear that not all goods are subject to this sort of demand. An individual obviously has no motive for an indirect exchange if he does not expect that it will bring him nearer to his ultimate objective, the acquisition of goods for his own use. The mere fact that there would be no exchanging unless it was indirect could not induce individuals to engage in indirect exchange if they secured no immediate personal advantage from it. Direct exchange being impossible, and indirect exchange being purposeless from the individual point of view, no exchange would take place at all. Individuals have recourse to indirect exchange only when they profit by it; that is, only when the goods they acquire are more marketable than those which they surrender.

Now all goods are not equally marketable. While there is only a limited and occasional demand for certain goods, that for others is more general and constant. Consequently, those who bring goods of the first kind to market in order to exchange them for goods that they need themselves have as a rule a smaller prospect of success than those who offer goods of the second kind. If, however, they exchange their relatively unmarketable goods for such as are more

---

2   The conclusion that indirect exchange is necessary in the majority of cases is extremely obvious. As we should expect, it is among the earliest discoveries of economics. We find it clearly expressed in the famous fragment of the Pandects of Paulus: "Quia non semper nec facile concurrebat, ut, cum tu haberas, quod ego desiderarem, invicem haberem, quod tu accipere velles" (Paulus, lib. 33 ad edictum 1.I pr. D. de contr. empt. 18, I).

Schumpeter is surely mistaken in thinking that the necessity for money can be proved solely from the assumption of indirect exchange (see his *Wesen und Hauptinhalt der theoretischen Nationalökonomie* [Leipzig, 1908], pp. 273 ff.). On this point, cf. Weiss, *Die moderne Tendenz in der Lehre vom Geldwert, Zeitschrift für Volkswirtschaft, Sozialpolitik und Verwaltung*, vol. 19, pp. 518 ff.

marketable, they will get a step nearer to their goal and may hope to reach it more surely and economically than if they had restricted themselves to direct exchange.

It was in this way that those goods that were originally the most marketable became common media of exchange; that is, goods into which all sellers of other goods first converted their wares and which it paid every would-be buyer of any other commodity to acquire first. And as soon as those commodities that were relatively most marketable had become common media of exchange, there was an increase in the difference between their marketability and that of all other commodities, and this in its turn further strengthened and broadened their position as media of exchange.[3]

Thus the requirements of the market have gradually led to the selection of certain commodities as common media of exchange. The group of commodities from which these were drawn was originally large, and differed from country to country; but it has more and more contracted. Whenever a direct exchange seemed out of the question, each of the parties to a transaction would naturally endeavor to exchange his superfluous commodities, not merely for more marketable commodities in general, but for the *most* marketable commodities; and among these again he would naturally prefer whichever particular commodity was the most marketable of all. The greater the marketability of the goods first acquired in indirect exchange, the greater would be the prospect of being able to reach the ultimate objective without further maneuvering. Thus there would be an inevitable tendency for the less marketable of the series of goods used as media of exchange to be one by one rejected until at last only a single commodity remained, which was universally employed as a medium of exchange; in a word, money.

This stage of development in the use of media of exchange, the exclusive employment of a single economic good, is not yet completely attained. In quite early times, sooner in some places

---

3   See Menger, *Untersuchungen über die Methode der Sozialwissenschaften und der politischen Ökonomie insbesondere* (Leipzig, 1883), pp. 172 ff.; *Grundsätze der Volkswirtschaftslehre*, 2d ed. (Vienna, 1923), pp. 247 ff.

than in others, the extension of indirect exchange led to the employment of the two precious metals gold and silver as common media
of exchange. But then there was a long interruption in the steady
contraction of the group of goods employed for that purpose. For
hundreds, even thousands, of years the choice of mankind has
wavered undecided between gold and silver The chief cause of this
remarkable phenomenon is to be found in the natural qualities of
the two metals. Being physically and chemically very similar, they
are almost equally serviceable for the satisfaction of human wants.
For the manufacture of ornaments and jewelry of all kinds the
one has proved as good as the other. (It is only in recent times that
technological discoveries have been made which have considerably
extended the range of uses of the precious metals and may have
differentiated their utility more sharply.) In isolated communities,
the employment of one or the other metal as sole common medium
of exchange has occasionally been achieved, but this short-lived
unity has always been lost again as soon as the isolation of the community has succumbed to participation in international trade.

Economic history is the story of the gradual extension of the
economic community beyond its original limits of the single household to embrace the nation and then the world. But every increase in
its size has led to a fresh duality of the medium of exchange whenever the two amalgamating communities have not had the same sort
of money. It would not be possible for the final verdict to be pro-
nounced until all the chief parts of the inhabited earth formed a
single commercial area, for not until then would it be impossible for
other nations with different monetary systems to join in and modify
the international organization.

Of course, if two or more economic goods had exactly the
same marketability, so that none of them was superior to the others
as a medium of exchange, this would limit the development toward
a unified monetary system. We shall not attempt to decide whether
this assumption holds good of the two precious metals gold and
silver. The question, about which a bitter controversy has raged for
decades, has no very important bearings upon the theory of the

nature of money. For it is quite certain that even if a motive had not been provided by the unequal marketability of the goods used as media of exchange, unification would still have seemed a desirable aim for monetary policy. The simultaneous use of several kinds of money involves so many disadvantages and so complicates the technique of exchange that the endeavor to unify the monetary system would certainly have been made in any case.

The theory of money must take into consideration all that is implied in the functioning of several kinds of money side by side. Only where its conclusions are unlikely to be affected one way or the other, may it proceed from the assumption that a single good is employed as common medium of exchange. Elsewhere, it must take account of the simultaneous use of several media of exchange. To neglect this would be to shirk one of its most difficult tasks.

The "Secondary" Functions of Money

The simple statement, that money is a commodity whose economic function is to facilitate the interchange of goods and services, does not satisfy those writers who are interested rather in the accumulation of material than in the increase of knowledge. Many investigators imagine that insufficient attention is devoted to the remarkable part played by money in economic life if it is merely credited with the function of being a medium of exchange; they do not think that due regard has been paid to the significance of money until they have enumerated half a dozen further "functions"—as if, in an economic order founded on the exchange of goods, there could be a more important function than that of the common medium of exchange.

After Menger's review of the question, further discussion of the connection between the secondary functions of money and its basic function should be unnecessary.[4] Nevertheless, certain tendencies in recent literature on money make it appear advisable to examine briefly these secondary functions—some of them are coordinated

---

4   See Menger, *Grundsätze*, pp. 278 ff.

with the basic function by many writers—and to show once more that all of them can be deduced from the function of money as a common medium of exchange.

This applies in the first place to the function fulfilled by money *in facilitating credit transactions*. It is simplest to regard this as part of its function as medium of exchange. Credit transactions are in fact nothing but the exchange of present goods against future goods. Frequent reference is made in English and American writings to a function of money as a standard of deferred payments.[5] But the original purpose of this expression was not to contrast a particular function of money with its ordinary economic function, but merely to simplify discussions about the influence of changes in the value of money upon the real amount of money debts. It serves this purpose admirably. But it should be pointed out that its use has led many writers to deal with the problems connected with the general economic consequences of changes in the value of money merely from the point of view of modifications in existing debt relations and to overlook their significance in all other connections.

The functions of money *as a transmitter of value through time and space* may also be directly traced back to its function as medium of exchange. Menger has pointed out that the special suitability of goods for hoarding, and their consequent widespread employment for this purpose, has been one of the most important causes of their increased marketability and therefore of their qualification as media of exchange.[6] As soon as the practice of employing a certain economic good as a medium of exchange becomes general, people begin to store up this good in preference to others. In fact, hoarding as a form of investment plays no great part in our present stage of economic development, its place having been taken by the purchase

---

5   See Nicholson, *A Treatise on Money and Essays on Present Monetary Problems* (Edinburgh, 1888), pp. 22 ff.; Laughlin, *The Principles of Money* (London, 1903), pp. 22 f.

6   Cf. Menger, *Grundsätze*, pp. 284 ff.

of interest-bearing property.[7] On the other hand, money still functions today as a means for transporting value through space.[8] This
function again is nothing but a matter of facilitating the exchange of
goods. The European farmer who emigrates to America and wishes
to exchange his property in Europe for a property in America, sells
the former, goes to America with the money (or a bill payable in
money), and there purchases his new homestead. Here we have an
absolute textbook example of an exchange facilitated by money.

Particular attention has been devoted, especially in recent
times, to the function of money *as a general medium of payment*. Indirect
exchange divides a single transaction into two separate parts which
are connected merely by the ultimate intention of the exchangers
to acquire consumption goods. Sale and purchase thus apparently
become independent of each other Furthermore, if the two parties
to a sale-and-purchase transaction perform their respective parts of
the bargain at different times, that of the seller preceding that of the
buyer (purchase on credit), then the settlement of the bargain, or the
fulfillment of the seller's part of it (which need not be the same thing),
has no obvious connection with the fulfillment of the buyer's part.
The same is true of all other credit transactions, especially of the
most important sort of credit transaction—lending. The apparent
lack of a connection between the two parts of the single transaction has been taken as a reason for regarding them as independent
proceedings, for speaking of the payment as an independent legal
act, and consequently for attributing to money the function of being
a common medium of *payment*. This is obviously incorrect. "If the
function of money as an object which facilitates dealings in commodities and capital is kept in mind, a function that includes the
payment of money prices and repayment of loans...there remains

---

7   That is, apart from the exceptional propensity to hoard gold, silver, and
     foreign bills, encouraged by inflation and the laws enacted to further it.

8   Knies in particular (*Geld und Kredit*, 2d ed. [Berlin, 1885], vol. 1, pp. 233 ff.)
     has laid stress upon the function of money as interlocal transmitter of value.

neither necessity nor justification for further discussion of a special employment, or even function of money, as a medium of payment."[9]

The root of this error (as of many other errors in economics) must be sought in the uncritical acceptance of juristical conceptions and habits of thought. From the point of view of the law, outstanding debt is a subject which can and must be considered in isolation and entirely (or at least to some extent) without reference to the origin of the obligation to pay. Of course, in law as well as in economics, money is only the common medium of exchange. But the principal, although not exclusive, motive of the law for concerning itself with money is the problem of payment. When it seeks to answer the question, What is money? it is in order to determine how monetary liabilities can be discharged. For the jurist, money is a medium of payment. The economist, to whom the problem of money presents a different aspect, may not adopt this point of view if he does not wish at the very outset to prejudice his prospects of contributing to the advancement of economic theory.

---

9   Cf. Menger, *Grundsätze*, pp. 282 f.

LUDWIG VON MISES

From "The Gold Problem" in
Planning for Freedom: Let the Market System Work

The Gold Problem

Why have a monetary system based on gold? Because, as conditions are today and for the time that can be foreseen today, the gold standard alone makes the determination of money's purchasing power independent of the ambitions and machinations of governments, of dictators, of political parties, and of pressure groups. The gold standard alone is what the nineteenth-century freedom-loving leaders (who championed representative government, civil liberties, and prosperity for all) called "sound money."

The eminence and usefulness of the gold standard consists in the fact that it makes the supply of money depend on the profitability

Ludwig von Mises, "The Gold Problem," in *Planning for Freedom: Let the Market System Work* (Indianapolis: Liberty Fund, 2008). See also the Liberty Fund— http://oll.libertyfund.org/titles/mises-planning-for-freedom-let-the-market-system-work-a-collection-of-essays-and-addresses.

of mining gold, and thus checks large-scale inflationary ventures on the part of governments.

The gold standard did not fail. Governments deliberately sabotaged it, and still go on sabotaging it. But no government is powerful enough to destroy the gold standard so long as the market economy is not entirely suppressed by the establishment of socialism in every part of the world.

Governments believe that it is the gold standard's fault alone that their inflationary schemes not only fail to produce the expected benefits, but unavoidably bring about conditions that (also in the eyes of the rulers themselves and most of the people) are considered as much worse than the alleged or real evils they were designed to eliminate. Except for the gold standard, governments are told by pseudo-economists that they could make everybody perfectly prosperous. Let us test the three doctrines advanced for the support of this fable of government omnipotence.

The Fiction of Government Omnipotence

"The state is God," said Ferdinand Lassalle, the founder of the German socialist movement. As such, the state has the power to "create" unlimited quantities of money and thus to make everybody happy. Intrepid and clear-headed people branded such a policy of "creating" money as inflation. The official terminology calls it nowadays "deficit spending."

But whatever the name used in dealing with this phenomenon may be, its meaning is obvious. The government increases the quantity of money in circulation. Then a greater quantity of money "chases" (as a rather silly but popular way of talking about these problems says) a quantity of goods and services that has not been increased. The government's action did not add anything to the available amount of useful things and services. It merely made the prices paid for them soar.

If the government wishes to raise the income of some people, for example, government employees, it has to confiscate by taxation a part of some other people's incomes, and then distribute the amount collected to its employees or favored groups. Then the taxpayers are forced to restrict their spending, while the recipients of the higher salaries or benefits are increasing their spending to the same amount. There does not result a conspicuous change in the purchasing power of the monetary unit.

But if the government provides the money it wants for the payment of higher salaries by printing it or the granting of additional credits, the new money in the hands of these beneficiaries constitutes on the market an additional demand for the not-increased quantity of goods and services offered for sale. The unavoidable result is a general tendency of prices to rise.

Any attempts the governments and their propaganda offices make to conceal this concatenation of events are in vain. Deficit spending means increasing the quantity of money in circulation. That the official terminology avoids calling it inflation is of no avail whatever.

The government and its chiefs do not have the powers of the mythical Santa Claus. They cannot spend except by taking out of the pockets of some people for the benefit of others.

The "Cheap-Money" Fallacy

Interest is the difference in the valuation of present goods and future goods; it is the discount in the valuation of future goods as against that of present goods. Interest cannot be "abolished" as long as people prefer an apple available today to an apple available only in a year, in ten years, or in a hundred years.

The height of the originary rate of interest, which is the main component of the market rate of interest as determined on the loan market, reflects the difference in the people's valuation of present and future satisfaction of needs. The disappearance of interest, that is, an interest rate of zero, would mean that people do not care a whit about satisfying any of their present wants and are *exclusively* intent upon satisfying their future wants, their wants of the later years, decades, and centuries to come. People would only save and invest and would not be consuming.

On the other hand, if people were to stop saving, that is, making any provision for the future, be it even the future of the tomorrow, and would not save at all and consume all capital goods accumulated by previous generations, the rate of interest would rise beyond any limits.

It is thus obvious that the height of the market rate of interest ultimately does not depend on the whims, fancies, and pecuniary interests of the personnel operating the government apparatus of coercion and compulsion, the much-referred-to "public sector" of the economy. But the government has the power to push the Federal Reserve System, and the banks subject to it, into a policy of cheap money. Then the banks are expanding credit. Underbidding the rate of interest as established on the not-manipulated loan market, they offer additional credit created out of nothing. Thus they are inescapably falsifying the businessmen's estimation of market conditions. Although the supply of capital goods (that can only be increased by additional saving) remained unchanged, the illusion of a richer supply of capital is conjured up. Business is induced to embark upon projects which a sober calculation, not misled by the cheap-money ventures, would have disclosed as mal-investments (over-investment in capital). The additional quantities of credit inundating the market make prices and wages soar. An artificial boom, a boom built entirely upon the illusions of ample and easy money, develops. But such a boom cannot last. Sooner or later it must become clear that, under the illusions created by the credit expansion, business has embarked upon projects for the execution of which the real savings are not rich enough. When this mal-investment becomes visible, the boom collapses.

The depression that follows is the process of liquidating the errors committed in the excesses of the artificial boom; it is the return to calm reasoning and a reasonable conduct of affairs within the limits of the available supply of capital goods. It is a painful process, but it is a process of restoration of business health.

Credit expansion is not a nostrum to make people happy. The boom it engenders must inevitably lead to a debacle and unhappiness.

If it were really possible to substitute credit expansion (cheap money) for the accumulation of capital goods by saving, there would not be any poverty in the world. The economically backward nations would not have to complain about the insufficiency of their capital equipment. All they would have to do for the improvement of their conditions would be to expand money and credit more and more. No "foreign aid" schemes would have emerged. But in granting foreign aid to the backward nations, the American government implicitly acknowledges that credit expansion is no real substitute for genuine capital accumulation through saving.

The Failure of Minimum Wage Legislation and of Union Coercion

The height of wage rates is determined by the consumers' appraisal of the value the worker's labor adds to the value of the article available for sale. As the immense majority of the consumers are themselves earners of wages and salaries, this means that the determination of the compensation for work and services rendered is made by the same kind of people who are receiving these wages and salaries. The fat earnings of the movie star and the boxing champion are provided by the welders, street sweepers, and charwomen who attend the performances and matches.

An entrepreneur who would try to pay a hired man less than the amount this man's work adds to the value of the product would be priced out of the labor market by the competition of other entrepreneurs eager to earn money. On the other hand, no entrepreneur can pay more to his helpers than the amount the consumers are prepared to refund to him in buying the product. If he were to pay higher wages, he would suffer losses and would be ejected from the ranks of the businessmen.

Governments decreeing minimum wage laws above the level of the market rates restrict the number of hands that can find jobs.

Such governments are producing unemployment of a part of the labor force. The same is true for what is euphemistically called "collective bargaining."

The only difference between the two methods concerns the apparatus enforcing the minimum wage. The government enforces its orders in resorting to policemen and prison guards. The unions "picket." They and their members and officials have acquired the power and the right to commit wrongs to person and property, to deprive individuals of the means of earning a livelihood, and to commit many other acts which no one can do with impunity. Nobody is today in a position to disobey an order issued by a union. To the employers no other choice is left than either to surrender to the dictates of the unions or to go out of business.

But governments and unions are impotent against economic law. Violence can prevent the employers from hiring help at potential market rates, but it cannot force them to employ all those who are anxious to get jobs. The result of the governments' and the unions' meddling with the height of wage rates cannot be anything else than an incessant increase in the number of unemployed.

It is precisely to prevent this outcome that the government-manipulated banking systems of all Western nations are resorting to inflation. Increasing the quantity of money in circulation and thereby lowering the purchasing power of the monetary unit, they are cutting down the oversized payrolls to a height consonant with the state of the market. This is today called Keynesian full-employment policy. It is in fact a method to perpetuate by continued inflation the futile attempts of governments and labor unions to meddle with the conditions of the labor market. As soon as the progress of inflation has adjusted wage rates so far as to avoid a spread of unemployment, government and unions resume with renewed zeal their ventures to raise wage rates above the level at which every job-seeker can find a job.

The experience of this age of the New Deal, the Fair Deal, the New Frontier, and the Great Society confirms the fundamental thesis of the true British lovers of political liberty in the nineteenth century, namely, that there is but one means to improve the material conditions of all of the wage earners, viz., to increase the per-head quota of real capital invested. This result can only be brought about by additional saving and capital accumulation, never by government decrees, labor-union violence and intimidation, and inflation. The foes of the gold standard are wrong also in this regard.

The Inescapable Consequence, Namely, the United States Government Gold Holdings Will Shrink

In many parts of the earth an increasing number of people realize that the United States and most of the other nations are firmly committed to a policy of progressing inflation. They have learned enough from the experience of the recent decades to conclude that on account of these inflationary policies an ounce of gold will one day become more expensive in terms both the currency of the United States and of their own country. They are alarmed and would like to avoid being victimized by this outcome.

Americans are forbidden to own gold coins and gold ingots. Their attempts to protect their financial assets consist in the methods that the Germans in the most spectacular inflation that history knows called *Flucht in die Sachwerte* (flight into real values). They are investing in common stocks and real estate, and prefer to have debts payable in legal tender money rather than holding claims payable in it.

Even in the countries in which people are free to buy gold there are up to now no conspicuous purchases of gold on the part of financially potent individuals and institutions. Up to the moment at which French agencies began to buy gold, the buyers of gold were mostly people with modest incomes anxious to keep a few gold coins as a reserve for rainy days. It was the purchases via the London gold market on the part of such people that reduced the gold holdings of the United States.

• • •

There is only one method available to prevent a further reduction of the American gold reserve, namely, radical abandonment of deficit spending as well as of any kind of "easy-money" policy.